THE MÉTIS
CANADA'S FORGOTTEN PEOPLE

D. BRUCE SEALEY
ANTOINE S. LUSSIER

Illustrations by Real Bérard

PEMMICAN
PUBLICATIONS
34 Carlton Street, Winnipeg
Manitoba, Canada R3C 1N9

Standard Book No. 0-919213-39-1

32,015

First Printing 1975
Second Printing 1975
Third Printing 1977
Fourth Printing 1979
Fifth Printing 1981

**PEMMICAN
PUBLICATIONS**
34 Carlton Street, Winnipeg
Manitoba, Canada R3C 1N9

To

MARGARET

mentor, colleague, friend, wife

PREFACE

M. E. de Montaigne (1533-92) ended a lecture by saying, "All I have done is make a bouquet from flowers already picked adding nothing but the string to tie them together." This is what has been attempted in *The Métis, Canada's Forgotten People*. No historical survey of the Metis has yet been written in English. It is hoped that this volume will meet the needs of diverse groups of readers.

Much has been written about the Métis but such efforts tend to center around Louis Riel, the insurrection in Red River in 1869-70 and the 1885 rebellion in the Northwest. To the student, the Métis and Louis Riel suddenly appear and as quickly disappear in most histories of Canada. This book is the history, not of one man or several incidents in history, but of a people.

The Métis appeared early on the pages of Canada's history, were a major determinant in the westward expansion of the nation and are still a significant segment of modern Canadian society. This book traces their origin and their slow evolution to nationhood; examines the Golden Age; describes the battles won and lost with the nation of Canada; follows their exodus and dispersion; takes the reader into that black period of Canadian history when the Métis were persecuted and blatantly discriminated against; sets the stage for their resurgence as a people and describes some of the problems they still face.

The Métis are Canada's forgotten people. It is the authors' hope that this book will help to arouse an awareness of them amongst the other members of Canadian society. This, then, is the justification of the study.

ACKNOWLEDGEMENTS

The authors acknowledge their reliance on the works of the following historians: Marcel Giraud, *le métis canadien: son role dans l'histoire de provinces de l'Ouest:* G. F. G. Stanley, *The Birth of Western Canada,* and *Louis Riel*; W. L. Morton, *Manitoba, A History*; Alexander Begg, *History of the North West* and *The Creation of Manitoba*; Isaac Cowie, *The Company of Adventurers*; M. A. MacLeod, *Cuthbert Grant of Grantown*; A. H. Tremaudain, *Histoire de la nation métisse dans l'Ouest Canadien.* Other books and archival material are acknowledged in the Chapter Notes.

A. S. Lussier wrote chapters four, five and six and D. B. Sealey was the author of chapters one, two, three, seven, nine, ten, eleven and twelve. Chapter eight was a joint effort. Responsibility for any errors of fact is accepted jointly by the authors. The interpretation of historical events is accepted individually on the basis of the authorship of the chapters noted above. The authors gratefully acknowledge the many people who assisted in the preparation of the book. The staff of the Manitoba Provincial Archives and the Provincial Library personnel were always co-operative, helpful and interested. Mr. Angus Spence, President of the Manitoba Métis Federation (1970-74), and the Director of Education, J. G. Chartrand, were helpful in dealing with the modern period. Mr. Ferdinand Guiboche, present President of the Métis Federation, offered valuable encouragement.

Above all others the perceptive comments and detailed editing of the manuscript by Colin Davies has contributed to a smoothly flowing narrative.

The book is better for the critical comments and meticulous proof reading done by Margaret Sealey. The monotonous typing and re-typing of first, second, third and fourth drafts of the manuscript, which is essential to the progress of any book, was done by Margaret Sealey, Leslie Langlois, Audrey Brown and Dawn Sealey. Dawn Sealey in particular laboured long hours at the typewriter and brought to the manuscript an enthusiasm that can be generated only by a sixteen year old girl. To all these people the authors express their appreciation.

With
special thanks to Dr. G. F. G. Stanley

TABLE OF CONTENTS

1

Origin of the
Métis

When the Europeans first came in contact with the Indians of Canada, it was always as a group of European sailors meeting a mixed male and female population. Sailors, separated from women during a long ocean voyage, formed alliances with native women as rapidly as possible. Sometimes marriages were quickly arranged; sometimes women were bought; sometimes they were kidnapped; but whatever the method, women were obtained. A standard answer of the Métis people to those curious as to when the Métis originated has been: "Nine months after the first White man set foot in Canada". It is an historically correct answer.

People of mixed-blood are known by different names throughout the world. White and Negro give mulatto; the white, yellow and black amalgam is a malay; the European and a Hindu is called a half-caste. The English language originally described a person of mixed British and Indian as a half-breed. As the mixed-bloods intermarried with the aborigines or White people, the fractions of mixtures became complex. At first, the mixtures were half-breeds, quarter-breeds, and eighth-breeds, but soon a fractional classification became impossible. In Canada this led the people to use the French word, "Métis", to describe the mixed-blood people. "Métis" was a term originally used by the French-speaking population in the North-west of North America to designate persons of White and Indian blood. In the South-west of North America, in Central and South America the term used is the Spanish word "Mestizo". Both derive from the Latin word

1

"miscere — to mix". Its most common spellings are métis, maitiff, mustees and mestizo. In Canada the term "Métis" is loosely applied to all persons of mixed White and Indian blood who are not classified as "Indian" by the government of the country. Such a use of the word was, at one time, used mainly in the West, as mixed-bloods of the East tended to be absorbed rapidly into either Indian tribes or European society. Those not absorbed were referred to as "non-status", which meant that such people were of Indian ancestry but did not have the legal status of an Indian. However since 1967, the term "Métis" has come into more extensive use in all parts of Canada and now is considered synonymous with half-breed.

As an identifiable group who aspired to nationhood, the Métis of Western Canada loom large in history books. The Métis were the principal determinant of Canada's expansion westwards. They created a new province, were instrumental in the incorporation of the West into Canada rather than into the United States and, until 1885, were the prime economic force in western Canada. Yet their role in history has been largely misunderstood by Canadians at large and often by the Métis people themselves. Too often their insurrections under Louis Riel have been considered as one individual's meteoric rise and fall and considered in relative isolation from the history of the Métis people. Little is known of their slow development as a people; their gradual rise to power in the West and their rapid decline. Still less appreciated is the fact that the Métis are still here as an identifiable group with hopes and aspirations that may yet prove embarrassing to Canada.

In most parts of the world, mixed-blood people have been considered socially and intellectually inferior to the dominant race. This has brought about a desire in many of them to escape into either the aboriginal or Euro-Canadian groups. In Canada some of those who merged with the Indians keep the White part as secret as possible, for fear of reprisals and social ostracism from Indian friends, neighbors and kin. Many of those who merged into the Euro-Canadian society keep the Indian part secret because of similar fears, which are increased by the unfavorable image usually held of aborigines by a sophisticated and technologically superior group. Only in the Northwest did the mixed-bloods emerge as a dominant group with an identifiable history and culture uniquely their own.

2

To untangle the web of history during the early development of the Métis people is difficult. Only the European had the secret of indelibly recording his views, actions and perceptions on paper. The unfolding of the early history of the Métis people necessarily depends upon the diaries, letters and journals kept by early explorers, traders and missionaries or upon information contained in the records of official boards and legislative acts. These records indicate that the development of people of mixed-blood followed different courses in Eastern and Western Canada. In the East, large numbers of mixed-bloods were rapidly assimilated into the dominant society.

The following excerpts from a scholarly publication of the Canadian government yields some clues as to the origins of mixed-bloods in Eastern Canada and the interior of the United States:

> Some of the Algonquian tribes of Canada mingled considerably with the Europeans during the French period, both in the East and toward the Interior. As early as 1693 a member of the LaSalle expedition married the daughter of the chief of the Kaskaskia . . . Few French families in that part of the country are free from Indian blood . . .
> The tribes that have furnished the most mixed bloods are the Cree and the Chippewa, (Ojibwa/Saulteaux) . . .
> The peoples of the Iroquois stock have a large admixture of white blood, French and English, both from captives taken during the wars of the 17th and 18th centuries but by process of adoption, much favored by them . . . As compared with the Indian, the mixed-blood, so far as the investigations have shown, is taller, men exhibiting greater divergence than women.[1]

In 1886, Dr. D. Wilson, one of the early ethnologists, wrote of his studies in America and observed that few people living in Sault Ste. Marie had not some Indian blood in their veins. Subsequent investigation revealed that this was typical of most frontier settlements. He noted that in Eastern Canada he had recognized "the semi-Indian features" in people of all social levels.[2] Not until the twentieth century did the process of assimilation cease. Only in this century have mixed-blood people in Eastern Canada tended to be segregated from both Indian and White societies.

It was in Western Canada, however, where the intermixture took place in an area geographically and socially isolated from a dominant European society, that the Métis grew in numbers, flourished and began to think of themselves as neither European nor Indian but as a distinct and separate people.

White traders penetrated the west to seek out the beaver. Although many kinds of fur were purchased from the Indians the beaver was the most sought after, for men's styles in Europe demanded high felt hats. When it was discovered that the fur of the beaver matted easily to make a sturdy felt cloth, the price of beaver pelts rose dramatically and the merchants of Europe and New France formed fur-trading companies and financed individuals to seek out and buy beaver pelts. The supply of beaver in the East soon dwindled, so that Indian tribes spread north, west and south to find new trapping grounds. Sometimes following them, and often ahead of them, were the trading companies and the independent *coureurs de bois.*

In 1661, Radisson and Groseillers set out to trade in the untrapped area north and west of Lake Superior. They traded with the Cree and Ojibwa and, with their assistance, returned to Montreal with fur-laden canoes. The search for furs had succeeded in opening up canoe routes into an area previously unvisited. Unhappy with the taxes levied upon them by New France, they went to London and were financed by English merchants to trade in the area surrounding Hudson Bay. After a successful fur-trading expedition there was formed in 1670, The Company of Adventurers of England Trading into Hudson's Bay. The isolation of the Northwest was therefore interrupted on two fronts: through Hudson Bay and via river routes from Lake Superior. The traders from New France, most of whom were French, penetrated the interior via the canoe routes and slowly interfered with the Hudson's Bay Company's trading policy, which obliged the Indians to travel to Hudson Bay to trade. In order to regain some of the inland trade, Henry Kelsey, a clerk in the Hudson's Bay Company, was sent into the interior in 1690 for the dual purpose of exploration and trade. The resulting expansion of the trading posts into the interior in future generations brought about greater interaction between Indians and Europeans so that more mixed-blood children were born.

Desire for companionship was a reason for many of the alliances with Indian women. As the traders were constantly moving, the convenience of a wife in every village was also a factor. Many alliances were undertaken for commercial reasons since, by taking as wife the daughter of a headman in a village, certain trading loyalties would be obtained. It was expected that the new kin group — and a nomadic band was usually a large kin group — would trade with a relative rather than a strange trader. The primary reason, however, for having an Indian wife was simply one of survival. In a non-technological society most work was done by hand and to exist required teamwork

4

with clearly differentiated roles for men and women. Men were hunters, trappers and protectors. Women took the meat from the hunt and dried it or rendered the meat into pemmican. They gathered berries, dug nutritious roots, cared for gardens and small fields of grain in agricultural areas, dried and smoked fish, tanned hides, made clothes, collected firewood, cooked, bore children and were largely responsible for their upbringing. It was almost impossible for men to survive without women. Europeans soon learned this lesson and, for this reason as well as for others, eagerly took Indian women as mates.

In some cases the alliances were casual. In many others an abiding affection sprang up between the mates. Some traders took an Indian wife back to New France or Britain; however, as the woman was likely to be lonely, unable to speak the language and socially ostracized because of her origin, the move rarely proved to be a happy one. More often, the *coureur de bois* or member of a trading company took the Indian wife to share his room and board as long as he remained in the Northwest. Upon retirement, or when the man was recalled to civilization, the woman with her numerous children, existed as best she could with the help of charitable friends. One other choice was often made by the trader. He worked in the country as long as he was able and then retired to live out his life with wife and family beside a trading post.

The children of such a union were in an enviable position. They were both bilingual and bicultural. They knew the lifestyle of the Indians and, if not the total way of life of the white man, at least his frontier style. The more intelligent boys learned to read and write and were sought after as clerks by the local trading company. The others, through the father's connections, would have the preferred jobs such as interpreters, canoemen, fur packers and manual workmen around the fort. Those who could not secure such positions were able to enter trapping on a competitive basis with their Indian relatives. Such Métis became indispensable to the Indians, for through them the Indians could negotiate more effectively with local traders. Through them they had access to some of the technological knowledge of the White man. Indeed many of the early Métis were chosen as chiefs of tribes because their knowledge and understanding of White culture was so urgently needed by the Indians.

Some Europeans literally founded new tribes, as in the case of the Willow or Parkland People who now form a part of the Duck Lake Indian Agency in Saskatchewan. George Sutherland came from Scotland in 1790 as an employee of the Hudson's Bay Company. He took a Cree wife and, a few years later, left the employ of the Bay and lived independently on the prairie. Later he took two more wives and had twenty-seven children who grew to adulthood. These children took mates from the surrounding tribes but always returned to live with the Sutherland family group. Thus there developed a group who, although the language was Cree, did not consider themselves Indian or White but rather as Métis. There were many groups or tribes formed in a manner similar to the Sutherland band. Some, such as the Parkland People in Saskatchewan or the Lake of the Woods people in Ontario, negotiated land claims with the Government of Canada and, by signing treaties, became Indians in the legal sense.

As there were no white women in Rupert's Land, there were only two groups amongst which the Métis youth, who became employees of the traders as clerks, could find wives. They could seek a wife amongst females from other Métis families or from the Indians. As the Métis population increased it became easier to find girls who were Métis and slowly there began to emerge a fledgling people in the West who had a unique and observable social system and culture, which was a blend of European and Indian. A new nation was forming — a nation of people who perceived themselves as neither White nor Indian but as something quite distinct.

When did such people appear and at what time did a distinct cultural group begin to emerge in the West? It cannot be determined by a year, a decade or in a particular area of the Northwest. It evolved slowly and its evolution was marked by friction.

At first the Hudson's Bay Company censured men who cohabited with Indian women and the governor established punishments for employees who frequented Indian tents. Later, a regulation forbade Indian women to enter any fort but it was a losing battle. When Henry Kelsey returned triumphant as the first White man to have seen the prairies, a story recounts how he was told to leave his woman outside the gates of York Factory and to enter and report to the governor. Kelsey refused to enter unless accompanied by his Indian wife. Such attitudes on the part of the traders changed the emphasis in company rules. By 1770 the Hudson's Bay Company was insisting, by regulation, that the employees marry their Indian and Métis mates — either by Indian or British ceremony. In 1835 the Company ruled that, if an

6

employee returned to Britain, he must take his wife and children with him or else assign part of his pension towards his wife's upkeep if she were left behind. Such regulations were caused by economic need, tempered by Christian morality. Too many posts had become characterized by family groups of Métis abandoned by traders who had left the country. These groups often existed upon handouts from the Company, which became a serious drain upon the fur trade profits. The new regulations ensured that abandoned wives would have an independent income and also encouraged more stable family groups. It did much to create a cohesiveness amongst the Métis and the small pensions allowed many families to escape the poverty and squalor that plagued the Indians in years of famine.

Such restraints were not often imposed by the smaller trading companies and individual traders operating in competition with the Hudson's Bay Company. The smaller companies often gained their furs by placing undue emphasis upon alcohol as a major item of trade. The results of such trading in terms of dissension, violence and hatred caused the independent traders to move constantly. Such men tended to take Indian women whenever and wherever they pleased. A woman was changed as one changed a shirt. Children of such unions were the mother's responsibility and when abandoned she had nowhere to turn except to her Indian kin. More than two hundred years of such actions have given many of the treaty Indians of Western Canada almost as many White physical characteristics as Indian. Not all traders from the East were like this; the larger the company, the greater the sense of moral responsibility evident in the regulations under which their traders worked.

Distinctly Métis villages began to develop around many trading posts as early as the latter half of the eighteenth century. Prior to that, however, the mixed-bloods were already playing a role in history. Arthur Dobbs, in his book of 1744, obtained his information almost wholly from a Métis trader, Joseph La France. James Isham, the celebrated Hudson's Bay Company trader, when given the important job as governor of York Factory, was told that he must not rejoin his Indian wife and

> you do not harbor or entertain any Indian woman or women in our factory or permit others under you to do so.

Apparently the order was not heeded for Isham's will directed that all

7

his property be given his half-breed son, Charles. The company regulations were obviously ignored by the men in the field. One example of the rapid rate at which these first Métis rose to positions of influence in the Hudson's Bay Company is that of the half-breed, Moses Norton, who became governor of Churchill in 1759.

The rate of increase of mixed marriages was startling. David Thompson, Canada's great geographer, married a half-breed woman and had twelve children, most of whom lived to adulthood. At every little trading post the number of Métis increased dramatically, so that by 1800 most posts had a number of Métis homes grouped around the walls. The Métis were assisted in their spread throughout the west by the misfortune of the Indians who were decimated time and time again by contact with European diseases — especially smallpox and measles.

Although disease also ravaged the Métis, they were not as badly affected as the Indians. Perhaps the European genes carried some resistance to smallpox and measles. Perhaps their father passed on to them superior habits of sanitation. Perhaps living in clusters near trading posts gave them access to medicine which, although primitive, assisted somewhat in arresting the diseases. Whatever the causes, the Métis expanded and began to fill the spaces emptied by Indian deaths. They became the major buffalo hunters and rapidly occupied vacant trapping areas.

With an expanding population, the Métis were able to fill an economic need of fur trading companies which arose from the method of transportation necessary to the Northwest. Rivers and lakes were the first highways and the use of the canoe, indigenous to the country, was the major means of transport. Light, swift, easily built, and quickly repaired with local materials, it was ideal for transport where numerous portages were necessary because of waterfalls, rapids, and land connections between waterways. The canoe could carry freight into the country and furs out but it was not large enough to carry a sufficient supply of food for its occupants on a long journey. The fur trading companies overcame the problem by creating a string of supply depots across the country from Lake Superior west to the Rocky Mountains and north to the Arctic. The problem of stockpiling food at the supply depots grew acute — in fact, almost desperate — as the line of fur trade posts stretched westwards and northwards into non-agricultural lands. Food needs were met by harvesting the countless millions of buffalo roaming the plains. The buffalo meat, preserved as pemmican in Indian fashion, became the staple food of canoemen and traders. The burgeoning Métis population commercialized buffalo hunting and pemmican making to both their own and the fur trading companies' advantage. The plentiful supply of this concentrated food enabled the traders from the East to replenish their supplies and push on for a thousand miles into the rich fur areas of the woodlands north of the prairies. There was such complete reliance upon an annual supply of pemmican that, to a great extent, the fur trading companies encouraged the incipient nationalism of the Métis in order to ensure their friendship and, consequently, a continuing supply of food.

The Métis originated from the fur traders, grew and thrived on the needs of an expanding trade and, as will become apparent in ensuing chapters, became at times both a pawn in trade rivalry and a major factor in the development of the West. The Métis were not only of mixed-blood but of mixed-culture and their lifestyle depended upon the river, the hunt, the fur trade and a pattern of primitive agriculture suited to a semi-settled people. Their lifestyle was midway between that of the nomadic Indian food gatherers and that of the Europeans, the economic base of which was agriculture. The unique needs of the fur trade made such a lifestyle practicable, the incredible numbers of buffalo (possibly increasing in numbers as deaths from European diseases among the Indian people lessened hunting pressures) made it feasible, and the isolation of the region allowed it to evolve. The Métis multiplied, prospered and became a people with a unique culture. The isolation of the West allowed for their evolution, in contrast with the mixed-bloods of the East who were assimilated almost as quickly as miscegenation created them, into either the Indian or European cultures.

These Métis people are the true Natives of Canada. Indians and Europeans were immigrants — only the millennia separated their penetration into the New World. The meeting of the two races produced a mixture which was not from another land but whose sole roots were in the New World. Over the centuries they developed into a strong, vigorous, hybrid race that spread throughout the West and evolved into a nation. In Western Canada they made their stand against the advancing Europeans, fought well and lost. The evolution, the stand and the loss is one of the fascinating and tragic stories of North America. Their subsequent history, their constant seeking for a

9

place in Canadian society, their desire to enter it with the dignity of men imbued with a deep sense of history shows how a people, even a defeated and forgotten people, continually search for a future.

2

A New Lifestyle
Develops

The mixture of Indian and White races caused the Métis to develop a distinct way of life which was a remarkable adaptation of two cultures to the environment of the Northwest (or Rupert's Land as it was called from 1720 until 1870). What the early Métis were like and how they lived is a question that can only be answered through the eyes of White people who recorded their impressions. Early traders, missionaries and travellers categorized people according to their particular interests. In writing of the early Métis, travellers tended to describe the people as French half-breeds or English half-breeds according to language used. Missionaries described them as Roman Catholics, Protestants or pagans. Traders wrote of them as rich or poor (in terms of furs) or tended to describe them by geographical areas. Others divided them according to surnames. None of these methods was particularly accurate. The Métis largely intermarried within mixed-blood people but kept incorporating into their groups the children of the ever-increasing European-Indian unions. The language spoken bore little relationship to the surname. John Bruce was the first president of the National Committee of Métis formed in 1869 but spoke only French. Some people with French names were Protestant and spoke only English. Some people with English names were Catholic and spoke only French. Geographical residence was a doubtful criterion for the buffalo hunt might take a man and his family several thousand miles from their original area and in some cases a family might not return for several years. Neither Métis nor Indian recognized international boundary lines although Indians recognized and honored certain tribal geographical boundaries. Métis went where they wished and were found from Illinois to the far north. The most practical method of categorizing Métis is by their lifestyle.

There were three types of lifestyles which Métis people followed prior to 1825. One typified those who had secured permanent employment with the fur trading companies as clerks, interpreters, canoemen and packers. These had permanent homes close to trading posts. Though the men, on occasion, might have duties which took them from home for extended lengths of time, the family as such stayed permanently in one location. These families, settled close to people who were capable of educating, and often having had an educated forefather, produced many of the early Métis leaders.

A second lifestyle was followed by the semi-settled people who lived on small farms. Large gardens, small plots of grain and some livestock occupied them for part of the year. Portions of the summer were devoted to annual hunts of the buffalo which, depending upon the location of the herds, might take a few weeks or a few months. In other months some commercial freighting with Red River carts might be undertaken.

The third type of Métis were those who made their living as hunters and trappers. They followed the buffalo herds in summer as did their Indian brothers and during the winter trapped in areas holding a promise of plentiful furs. Home to these Métis was where they temporarily pitched a teepee or built a log shack.

In each of these three types there were to be found French speaking half-breeds and English speaking half-breeds. In one area, the Red River Settlement, there developed a relatively large group of English speaking half-breeds, most of whom were settled farmers, but this came about after the Selkirk Settlement was established in 1811.

The Ojibway Indians perhaps gave the best description of the mixed-bloods. They described them not as farmers, buffalo hunters, voyageurs, Métis or half-breeds but as "wissakodewinmi," meaning "half-burnt woodmen." The description of their lighter complexion, as compared with Indians, became shortened to "burnt wood" or "burnt sticks" and seemed apt. The French picked up the translation and the term "burnt wood — bois brûlé" came into current use.

G. Bryce reporting to the Royal Society of Canada in 1903 said of the Métis:

> ... the Metis or boisbrule became a well marked type in Rupert's Land. At the beginning of the 19th century, so decided had become the feeling of kinship and common interest that the boisbrule spoke of themselves as "The New Nation"[1] ...

Later Bryce writes of the English half-breed:

> So early as 1775, Alexander Henry, Sr. found Orkneymen in the company's service at Fort Cumberland. So largely did this element preponderate in the service that in 1816 we find the Bois brule speaking of the people of the company as "Les Orcanais". The Orkeymen largely intermarried with the Indian women in different parts of Rupert's Land, and usually on leaving the service settled near Fort Garry. Hence the socalled English half-breed, were only known as such on account of their language, but locally were usually called "Scotch half-breeds" . . . The names occurring amongst these people of mixed blood are Inkster, Tait, Setter, Fobister, Harper, Mowat, Omand, Flett, Linklater, Spence, Monkman, Isbister, Norquay, and so on.[2]

With the exception of the Red River settlement the Métis were close to fur trading posts. Their maternal background, the Indian, gave them a broad knowledge of the traditional ways. Yet their association with a White father gave them a competitive spirit, a knowledge of other ways, and often an access to the knowledge contained in books. Whether by himself or with the help of the father he began to improve upon the Indian way of life. This in itself represents a central theme in Canadian history — the contact of European civilization with the ancient cultures of the wilderness. The dominant question was how cultures and environment could be modified and this fundamental question was personified in the Métis. To observers at that time it seemed the choices were clear cut. The mixed-bloods could become nomads of the woods and plains or they could become as Europeans and be governed by the pen and the plough. The Métis chose neither one, but pulled both ways incessantly and sought a compromise between European and Indian ways; between paganism and Christianity; between hunting and agriculture.

The economics of the fur trade assisted in creating the ambivalence and it is within the economic stresses of the period 1812 — 1825 that an explanation can be found for the restless character of the Métis and the violent actions of 1816, 1849 1869 and even of 1885.

An examination of the observations written by Europeans who visited or lived in the West illustrated the types of accommodation being made.

From time immemorial the Indians had raised dogs. The use of them as beasts of burden was usually limited to attaching a light pack

15

which was carried on the back or hauling a load on a travois which consisted of two sticks which projected backwards from a collar and shoulder harness. The Métis, doubtlessly gaining the knowledge from their European fathers, soon harnessed the dogs to the Indian toboggan and adapted the European sleigh to a similar purpose. Apparently such a change in lifestyle for dogs was not altogether a happy circumstance for either dogs or men. The following quotation gives a sense of the problems involved for men and beast.

> The fact is, that in hauling, the dog is put to a work from which his whole nature revolts; that is to say the ordinary yellow dog. The result being, that just when one imagines everything to be going on swimmingly, and after he is well wrapped in robes and fairly seated in the sledge, the four yellow dogs in front of him suddenly stop, face about in harness, seat themselves calmly, and with tears in their dark-blue eyes, break forth into howls of regret at their inability to proceed farther. There have been men distinguished for kindness and humanity toward their fellows, and yet who, when placed in circumstances like these, gave way to a sublimated and lurid profanity which would have curled the hair on a bronze idol.[3]

The half-breeds, according to the same author, had made similar accommodations concerning Indian and European dress styles. The White men dressed thusly:

> He first puts on three or four flannel shirts, one of duffel, and over a leather one, beaded and fringed to suit the taste; his hands are encased in mittaines, or large gloves of moose-skin, made without fingers, and extending well up toward the elbows; loose enough to be easily doffed on occasion, and carried slung by a band about the neck to prevent being lost; his feet are swathed in duffel, and covered with enormous moccasins, his legs are encased in thick duffel leggins, until they resemble a severe case of elephantiasis; his ears and neck are protected by a thick curtain of fur; and yet; with it all, he is hardly able to keep warm with the most active exercise.[4]

Robinson says this about the half-breed clothing styles.

> Inured to climate and accustomed to winter travel, he is comfortable under a meagre weight of clothing. He relies upon vigorous exercise for the development of caloric and is constantly in motion. A pair of corduroy trousers, a cotton shirt, a capote, moccasins and a fur cap, constitute his winter costume. His hands are encased in mittaines, but in lieu of under clothing he ties his trousers tightly about the ankles, and the sleeves of his capote closely about the wrists. This, with the gaudy sash always wrapped around his waist, divides his clothing into two air-tight compartments, as it were. If it becomes cold in one, he always had the other in which to take refuge; or, he can loosen his belt, thus turning on a supply of caloric, which equalized the temperature in both compartments. Lightly clad, he is in excellent trim for running, and seems warm and comfortable while his more heavily appareled companion shakes and shivers on the slightest halt.[5]

16

All the men in the West were greatly impressed by one aspect of the Métis — their women. Cree women had been the favored choice of mates by fur traders. Generally slimmer and finer featured than those of other tribes, the Cree women were seen by many of the early traders as being closer to a European ideal of womanhood and thus more suitable as mates and mothers than members from other tribes. Apparently the mixing of European and Cree produced average men but beautiful women. The early travellers made constant reference to the Métis girls and phrases such as "glowing complections", "pearl-like teeth", "modest habits", "slim figures", "a flash of well turned ankle", "religious and chaste women", appear in journals and diaries. They reflected a European standard of beauty which would be eagerly sought for and duly appreciated by men far removed from home.

It was these women who, keeping the leather skills of their Indian ancestors, added the glass beads sold by the trading companies. They developed leatherwork into a superb craft, perhaps an art; they produced beaded moccasins, coats, belts and mittens for their man. The work was so beautiful that the beads were quickly adopted by the Indians who, previous to this, had decorated clothing mainly with intricately worked porcupine quills. It was the Métis women, who took the leather and furs of the country and made clothes with indigenous materials patterned on the European style of tailoring clothes to body shape. Rather than use the straight flowing robe of the Indian or share his habit of wrapping a huge blanket around himself, the Métis women tended to dress their families much as did the Europeans. From their European husbands they learned the art of making the simple unleavened bread which is still a staple food in Indian and Métis communities. This bread, called bannock, needed flour and the women quickly learned to pulverize the roots of certain western plants, especially the roots of common bulrushes and cattails, to use when wheat flour was not available.

Of a very religious nature, the women were a softening and refining influence on the Métis men, whose very mode of life tended to make them hard and callous. The influence of Métis women upon Indians was equally great, as Indian women quickly learned from their neighbors the craft of beading, making bannock and cooking in the newly introduced iron pots. The half-breed women thus played an important role in the accommodation of Indian and European cultures to each other.

17

Although impressed with some aspects of the lifestyle of Métis, Robinson was not impressed with them as farmers. He describes the Métis farmer as "not being fond of labor" and goes on to ascribe to this characteristic the unkempt look of many Métis farms. [6]

Robinson was equally unimpressed by their overcrowded homes but perhaps his bias is partially revealed when he speaks of "hospitality being a savage virtue."

> Caught one stormy winter's evening, on the banks of a northern river, without preparation for camping, our uncivilized guide halted before the door of a small cabin, and asked permission to stay overnight. Hospitality being one of the savage virtues, the request was readily granted. After a meagre supper of fish without salt, and a postprandial smoke, we began to look about for a couch for the night. Nothing was visible save one narrow bed, in which our host and his swarthy consort soon retired. Now, in addition to ourselves and guide, there were thirteen of the family, composed of children, male and female, from infancy to mature age. Where were they all to sleep? We thought of a possible loft; but there was no ceiling. Finally, we were about making preparations to sit before the fire all night when, from trunks and boxes were produced blankets and robes, and a shake-down made on the floor, into which we were directed to crawl. Scarcely had we done so, when our bed began to widen, and in a few minutes extended from wall to wall. Soon we found ourselves the central figure in a closely-packed bed of thirteen, filled promiscuously with males and females. [7]

One would assume a spirit of depression amongst the people who lived with large families in overcrowded log houses subsisting mainly on the chance of the hunt, with luxuries such as tea and sugar dependent upon the results of the trapline. Apparently just the opposite was noticeable. No group was happier than the Métis. Hardships and hunger were aspects of life they accepted rather than complained about. When groups of them came together in either a summer village or winter camp there was considerable merry making. Indeed, some traders felt the merry making went on so long that work was neglected.

Dancing was a favorite form of recreation. The Métis learned from their mothers the dances of the Plains Indians and the reels and square dances of Scotland from their fathers. They combined the intricate footwork of the Indians with the Scottish forms. The fiddle, a favorite of the Scots, became the beloved instrument of the Métis. Lacking the finances to buy imported European fiddles, they quickly learned to make their own from maple wood and birchbark. Some travellers sarcastically noted that lacking other instruments with which to tune the fiddles, the Métis used the cry of the loon and the bellow of a rutting moose. To the wild squeals of the homemade fiddles they developed a unique dance of their own — the Red River jig — which was a combination of Scottish jigs and Indian dance steps. It was one of the favorite dances and often a jig would start in early evening and, through the slow elimination of challengers, might not end until dawn. The jig steps were also incorporated into the square dances and even the French and English languages were intermixed in the directions shouted by a caller to the dancers. *A la main gauche* became *a la main left* and at dances all over Western and Northern Canada to this day, it can be heard in the distorted form of *allemande left*.

Though dancing occupied the nights, horse racing was the favorite daytime sport. Beribboned and prancing horses, either ridden by swash-buckling young men, or harnessed to gaily decorated carrioles, enlivened the road through a settlement in summer or the frozen river in winter. Challenges were readily given and accepted, most often with wagers on the outcome of the race. Everyone partook of the excitement except the dour Scotch people who, for generations, were shocked that the major races were often run on the Sabbath. Though poor — even destitute — the life of the Métis always had its good moments.

That the Métis were neither White nor Indian can be seen from the following phrases from many sources used to describe these mixed-bloods.

> For four days after birth the newly born infant receives no nourishment from the mother, in order that in after life it shall be able to withstand the pangs of hunger.
>
> The only thing given a new born child is a spoonful of whiskey in order to insure him a vigorous constitution in after life.
>
> It is impossible to enter the house of a half-breed without being asked to dine.
>
> A Métis maid wears a gaudy handkerchief upon her head but wears it meekly upon her breast when married.
>
> In courtship the young man commonly whispers endearments to his lover in three languages. He may call her a "muskox", in Cree, a "wolverine" in French but the standard and commonplace love name is said in English "my little pig."
>
> On the wedding day the man gives a present of a few ponies or a quantity of provisions to his prospective father-in-law.
>
> Members of a camp live in the most perfect socialist and communistic community in the world. Its members hold every article of food in common.

It is apparent from the above that one can trace both Indian and European traits in the Métis. Neither culture was predominant but customs from both rubbed against each other until something slightly different was produced which fit the environment perfectly.

In every aspect of life the Métis adjusted European technology to the prairies. The Indian had no knowledge of the wheel, but because of their European ancestry the Métis knew of it and some may have observed it in action as a means of transportation in vehicles in Eastern Canada, as well as in wheelbarrows at the larger fur posts. The cart that emerged as being so useful on the prairies was first developed in the Red River Valley. Yet, like most things associated with the Métis, it was not "invented". Rather it was a modification of the iron and wood carts common to Quebec. Alexander Henry, the younger, in charge of the North West Company post at Pembina described it in 1801.

> Men now go again for meat, with small carts, the wheels of which are one solid piece, sawed off the ends of trees whose diameter is three feet. Those carriages we find more convenient and advantageous than it is to load horses, the country being so smooth and level that we can use them in every direction.

As the years passed the cart became lighter and stronger. By 1820 it was described as being able to carry a load of five hundred pounds and, when pulled by a horse, travel fifty miles a day. If pulled by an ox, one thousand pounds could be carried for a distance of twenty miles a day. The wheels of the cart were "dished", that is, built in the shape of a saucer which assisted the broad wheel rim in not cutting as deeply into the soil as one which was perfectly flat. A box rested on the axle in which were carried the goods to be transported. When a river barred the progress of the cart the problem was solved by removing the wheels, attaching them under the axle and box, exclosing all this in a buffalo hide tarpaulin, and rafting the contraption across the water. The cart was made entirely of wood and its various parts bound together by wet rawhide which shrank after drying and was apparently as hard as iron. If at any time a breakdown should occur a nearby bluff of trees supplied the materials needed for repairs. Wood rubbing upon wood is one the world's least pleasant sounds but, despite the availability of grease or tallow in the west, the friction and resultant noise could not be reduced for, if greased, dust collected around the axle and this grit soon cut through the wood. The Métis learned to

20

accept the noise as a necessary evil but the travellers in the west invariably tried to describe what they referred to as an indescribable noise by using such phrases as "hellish", "unearthly", "ungodly", "horrifying", and "nerve-wracking". One Indian legend attributed the disappearance of the buffalo to a need to flee from the hideous noise made by the carts.

As the need for a greater amount of land transport developed, the Métis beame adept at putting many carts under one driver's control. The driver rode or walked beside the first cart and tied to the right hand rear of the cart would be a second ox and cart, and to the right hand rear of it would be a third ox and so on until the driver might be handling five oxen and carts. Thus a series of ruts was made in the grass rather than one, and the danger of sinking into the prairie in wet weather lessened. In addition, the possibility of getting hopelessly stuck in the bog was decreased, for if one cart became mired the others could be used to pull it out.

Soon a series of cart trails across the prairies rivalled the rivers as transportation routes. The first trails originated in Winnipeg and spread south and west. A major trail wound south from Winnipeg to Pembina and St. Paul. Westwards, the main trail wound along the Assiniboine to Portage la Prairie, split into three, converged again at Fort Ellice where it split again and rutted the prairie soil to Fort Pelly in the north and Fort Qu'Appelle to the west. From Qu'Appelle a trail led to the Cypress Hills while a second went through Batoche, Battleford, Fort Carlton and thence to Edmonton. Minor trails connected the main trails and to a great extent modern highways are built on the old cart trails of the Métis freighters. So common were the Métis with their carts that the Indians had a special way to describe them in the universal sign language of the plains: the fingers of each hand circling each other to represent cart wheels and then the finger drawn down in front of the body to represent the fraction one-half. Literally translated, the sign said a Métis was half-wagon, half-man.

Douglas Hill, a Canadian historian, commented that the opening of the west owed much to the existence of "these allround conveyances", in acknowledgement of the importance of the Métis carts.[8]

Exciting and romantic as carting may appear, the trials and tribulations of the Métis cart men were many. The swamps and sloughs of the prairie were greater in number before agricultural practices dried so much of the soil. The sloughs were the breeding grounds of mosquitoes and from them, if wind conditions were right, millions of the insects would be blown over the route traversed by a cart brigade. The cart train would be literally covered in a few seconds. Horses and oxen would scream in pain from savage bites and runaways were frequent. All the drivers could do was to lie, covered with blankets, on the ground until the worst of the hordes were blown away.

Prairie fires, however, were the greatest fear of the cart brigades. Not only did the heavily loaded carts have no chance of outrunning a grass fire but, if death by burning was avoided by fleeing to a nearby slough and partially immersing men and beasts in water, death from starvation was possible before unburned country containing grass and game could be reached.

Joseph Kinsey Howard expressed his admiration,

> These men and the captain of the whole train walked a thousand miles a season, endured tortures from insects, faced the hazards of storm and fire and the back-breaking labor of extricating the carts from gluey gumbo potholes, almost without complaint. They were traditionally as cheerful as their voyageur forebearers.[9]

One of the major changes that came about as a result of the Red River cart was a different method of harvesting the buffalo herds, which allowed these to be commercially exploited with greater ease. The key to commercialization was the cart, which allowed large quantities of pemmican to be transported hundreds of miles across the prairies. It also permitted the Métis to develop as a semi-settled people rather than remain nomadic.

In pre-European times, the Plains Indians had to follow the buffalo herds at all times to eke out a living, as the use of bows and arrows limited their hunting effectiveness, as did the lack of horses and the fact that they were in competition with wolves and grizzly bears for stragglers of the herd. Some insight into the pre-gun, pre-horse method of hunting buffalo can be had from reading an entry in the journal of Henry Kelsey, the first White man to see the buffalo. It is also the first description of a buffalo hunt and likely took place in the Swan River Valley of Manitoba.

> August Ye 23rd (1691) — This instant ye Indians going a hunting killed great store of Buffilo. Now ye manner of their hunting these Beast on ye barren ground is when they see a great parcel of them together they surround them with men wch done they gather themselves into a smaller

Compass keeping ye Beast still in ye middle and so shooting ym until they breatk out at some place or other and so get away from you.

With the introduction of horses by the Spanish, and their subsequent reversion to a wild state, the Plains Indians rapidly made the horse an important part of their culture. They soon became superb horsemen and masters of the buffalo and their competitors, the grizzlies and the wolves. No longer was it necessary to wait for the buffalo to come to them or follow the herd all year and stalk them on foot. The horse made the Indian absolute master of the plains and all upon it and removed the need for tagging along after the buffalo herds. Now it was possible for the tribe to range over hundreds of miles in a few days. With a plentiful and easily gathered supply of food, men had much free time and the culture of the Plains Indians became rich and unique. Now Indians had time to devote to the Arts, storytelling, philosophy and the expression of the innermost man through music and dance.

The multitude of buffalo around which Indians and Métis built a way of life was uncountable. There are records of awesome herds being observed by explorers and travellers. A party camped in Qu'Appelle Valley in Sasktachewan watched for twenty-four hours as animals forded the river at several hundred per minute. This herd alone was estimated to number over one million. In 1873, around the Cypress Hills area in Alberta, a party rode one hundred and fifty miles in a week and never got out of one vast herd of grazing buffalo. In 1874, the North West Mounted Police recorded eighty thousand in one herd. These records are amazing inasmuch as at this time the buffalo were reaching a point of extinction; by 1883 there were only one thousand buffalo left, largely in parks and private reserves.

The mind cannot comprehend the many millions of buffalo which roamed the plains of North America at the time covered in this chapter — approximately 1780-1810. Some historians have estimated that the plains must have been a vast pasture containing upwards of sixty million buffalo while others have estimated as high as one hundred million.

The Indians, with the advent of the horse, developed two basic methods of killing buffalo — the pound and the piskin. The pounds were giant log and brushwork corrals or dead-end *coulées* into which a herd was driven and systematically killed. The piskin or cliff method was one in which buffalo were stampeded in the direction of a precipituous cliff, often bordering a river valley. In their wild flight, forced forward by frightened thousands in the rear, the animals would fall over the cliff. At the bottom the Indians would move in on the writhing, bellowing animals held captive by broken bones, and mercifully kill them.

The Métis buffalo hunters usually used a method known as "running the herd". Scouts would locate a grazing herd and the Métis would slowly ride forward in formation. At a signal, the riders would gallop towards the herd, which would immediately stampede in fear. On their swift horses the men would ride through the mélee shooting prime buffalo cows as they swept past them. Passing through the herd, the men would turn their horses and "run" the herd again and again until a sufficient number of buffalo were killed. At all times the hunter was in great danger of being thrown from his horse, since his horse might collide with a buffalo or step into an animal burrow. Whatever the cause, if a man became unmounted, his chances of survival were slim indeed, for the stampeding herd would surely trample him. The guns, muzzle-loading types, were a danger in themselves. A man carried a powderhorn (made from a buffalo horn) and a mouth full of lead balls. As he rode at top speed through the herd it was necessary to pour powder into the muzzle of the gun, spit a lead ball in on top of it, pound the gun butt on his saddle to shake powder and lead down, select a fat cow, ride beside it, bring his gun down, point it at the heart of the buffalo, and fire. Still at a gallop amongst stampeding buffalo, a new cap was placed in the gun and the process began again. The danger of being hit by stray bullets; the possibility that the gun might explode and blow off fingers or a hand; the ever present fear of being gored by a buffalo horn; all these were part of the thrill of the hunt. The danger and excitement were necessary in order to gather a supply of meat with which to make pemmican.

Exciting the hunt may have been, but its success signalled the beginning of hard labor for the Métis women. After the kill the women took over as butchers. Meat was hauled back to the temporary camps in the Red River carts and there cut into thin slabs and hung on racks to dry in the sun. When dry it was baled. Later, if to be made into pemmican, it had to be beaten with sticks or stones until shredded. Mixed with hot buffalo fat and berries, if available, the mixture was poured into buffalo hide bags holding approximately one hundred pounds. When cool it hardened and an axe was usually used to cut off

24

chunks which were eaten raw or boiled. Pemmican kept for years and although tasteless it was nutritious and compact — one pound of pemmican was considered the equivalent of four pounds of fresh meat. It was this concentrated food which allowed canoes and carts to transport trade goods and furs for thousands of miles. It was pemmican that kept alive the trader in the isolated posts, as well as the trapper on the trapline. Deer, elk, moose, caribou or any kind of meat could be made into pemmican but these animals were not available in numbers large enough to meet the needs of the northern trade. Buffalo pemmican was the basis for the development of the West. The Métis hunt was an exciting spectacle, full of sound and furious activity, but it was more than that. The Métis were building it into a major business enterprise, the success of which allowed a long line of fur trading posts to exist and a thousand voyageurs in canoes or carts to transport trade goods and furs across a continent.

The development of carting, buffalo hunting and simple agriculture must not be allowed to obscure one of the oldest and most reliable forms of livelihood the Métis had — that of voyageurs and tripmen. The trade routes they travelled were the rivers and lakes — not only the pleasant lakes and placid rivers frequented by modern tourists — but also the turbulent rivers with rapids, waterfalls, backbreaking portages and through country notorious as the home of countless trillions of savage mosquitoes and flies. A seemingly glamorous job it was to travel the waterways of Canada, but these Métis voyageurs knew hardships that few men could tolerate. Sixteen to eighteen hours of daily labor, paddling canoes holding three tons of freight; the back-breaking labor of carrying one hundred and eighty pound loads through bogs, up rocky inclines and over long portages; lining (tracking) a canoe up rapids while immersed to the waist in ice-cold water; these were but a few of the hazards and hardships which characterized the daily work of a voyageur.

The portage was the least dangerous, but the most strenuous, part of a voyageur's work. It was made only as a last resort when the rapids or falls made a river impassable to canoe or when the route moved from one river to another and canoes and frieght had to be transported overland. With a view to the inevitable portages on every route, the freight goods were assembled in packs of ninety pounds each. One pack was put into a leather sling which was supported at the top of a man's forehead and hung down his back. On top of ninety pounds con-

25

tained in the sling was placed a second pack of equal weight. With this load, totaling one hundred eight pounds, the man, slightly bent, moved forward at a shuffling trot. While portaging, the expected rate of progress was one-half mile every ten minutes, followed by a short rest. The canoe, usually thirty-six feet long, was made of birchbark and, though relatively light in comparison with wooden boats, weighed six hundred pounds. It was portaged by four men — two at the bow and two at the stern — who carried it in inverted fashion on their shoulders In the rocky, rapids-ridden rivers of the northern areas a smaller twenty-five foot canoe, which weighed only three hundred pounds, was more common.

The most exciting, yet also the most dangerous, work of a voyageur was running navigable rapids. The speed of descent and the danger of hitting rocks created an excitement that must have been increased by an awareness of how fragile a birch bark canoe really was.

Up at two a.m.; a six hour paddle; breakfast at eight; lunch at noon, which consisted of a piece of pemmican hacked off and chewed while the paddling continued; supper at nine p.m. and then a few hours sleep in the open before beginning another day; this was the accepted schedule for a voyageur. One important ritual must not be forgotten. Every hour on the hour the paddling ceased and men lighted their pipes. Distance was measured by voyageurs in "pipes" and one stopped for a "pipe" every four or five miles. This method of measurement is still found in many Indian and Métis communities today and has been extended to land measurements as well. Thus a person today will sometimes say his trapline is thirty pipes long by twenty pipes wide.

The strenuous life led by the canoe men helps us to appreciate their vast appetites, at which modern man marvels and in his ignorance often considers as an example of Métis gluttony. The geographer and fur trader, David Thompson, noted that the daily ration for each voyageur consisted of either eight pounds of fresh meat a day or one and a half pounds of pemmican. Although few modern men could eat eight pounds of fresh meat a day they may be able to feel some of the exuberance of the voyageur as the stereo brings their rousing paddling songs to the living room. The spirit of the Métis canoe men is immortalized in songs such as *En rouland ma boule, C'est l'aviron* and *Youpe! Youpe! sur la rivère!* which have remained popular in the Canadian folk song heritage.

The birch back canoe, that marvellous invention of the Woodland Indians, had one drawback in that it lacked strength and durability. It was this weakness that caused the Hudson's Bay Company to abandon the use of the canoe on the route from York Factory on the Hudson Bay to Norway House, where it divided to go south to the Red River and west on the Saskatchewan River toward Edmonton. William Sinclair, a Métis, developed, in 1835, a new boat, often referred to as a man killer, which was slow but sturdy and capable of carrying more and heavier freight than the canoe. The cumbersome York boat was created for these specific transport routes. Too heavy to be carried, it had to be dragged over portages but this was balanced by the ease with which sails could be hoisted on days when the wind was suitable. The York boat was rowed or sailed rather than paddled, but many a weary Métis boatman swore that it was dragged more often then it moved under the first two means of power.

In 1819, Sir John Franklin wrote this vivid description of travel by York boat.

> On the 9th September our boat being completed, arrangements were made for our departure as soon as the tide should serve . . . The wind and tide failing at the distance of six miles above the York Factory, and the current being too rapid for using oars to advantage, the crew had to commence tracking, or dragging the boat by a line, to which they were harnessed. This operation is extremely laborious . . . Our men were obliged to walk along the steep declivity of a high bank, rendered at this season soft and slippery by frequent rains, and their progress was often further impeded by fallen trees.[10]

The commercial buffalo hunts, cart brigades, canoe and York boat transportation systems served several purposes, but their main reason for existence was to serve the fur trade. The fur trade existed because it met a need of people in Europe, where the beaver was in great demand because of felt hat styles. Other furs were trapped also — mink, martin, fisher, otter, ermine (weasel), fox and lynx, though coarser furs such as bear and wolf also found a market. Increasingly buffalo hides became popular as robes and blankets throughout the world and, for the Métis, an important source of income.

It was as a result of the collecting of furs that the Métis people came into existence and, in the early years, the fur trade or its supporting services was their life. Whether on a winter hunt for buffalo, driving Red River carts or working at a trading post, the Métis were constantly involved in the search for furs. Some trapped each year in a favorite area, others trapped when other jobs were not available. Many trapped as the Indians did. Others, who were attached to a fur trading post, spent most of the winter carrying food, ammunition and other trade goods by dog team from one camp to another. A return to the trading post was made only when the sleigh load of trading goods was gone. Both the North West Company and the Hudson's Bay Company depended to a great extent upon the services of the Métis who acted as middlemen. Slowly, the more aggressive Métis became independent and began to operate as private or "free" traders. The two large fur companies were not unduly concerned, as they would receive the furs either by purchase from trappers themselves or from the small trader. Nevertheless, the development of leading Métis people as small businessmen, whether as cart men, canoe and York boat men who contracted to deliver goods, or as semi-independent fur traders, was laying the ground for serious trouble in future generations. Once trade routes were opened to towns in the United States, the continued prosperity of the Hudson's Bay Company would demand that the independent trading by Métis be curbed. As events will show, it is extremely difficult to try and deny a man something which his historical tradition tells him is his right.

As buffalo hunters, canoe trippers, York boat men, carters or small farmers the Métis people led a hard, hazardous life and prospered. With so many dangers as a part of everyday life it is little wonder they followed their Indian brothers in living for the present, rather than planning for the future. They opened the country, earned a living as best they could, were successful in adapting to the country when forced to, but mastered it when possible.

They were independent, asked no favors from either Indians or Europeans, but developed as men of dignity and earned respect, albeit grudgingly given at times, from both parent groups.

Although most were illiterate, or poorly educated at best, some received a good education in other lands. Scottish or French fathers would often send at least one dusky son home to be educated in Scotland or Canada (which, at that time, consisted of what is now Ontario and Quebec) respectively. Many of these educated men returned to the West and provided leadership and guidance to the Métis. Cuthbert Grant and Louis Riel are prime examples of such men. Others, having left the West, still worked for the Métis people, though in different countries. Alexander Kennedy Isbister, a Métis born at

Cumberland House, lived in the west for twenty years and then went to England to gain a higher education. He became an outstanding barrister and educator. In the legal battles the Métis were to have later with the Hudson's Bay Company, it was Isbister who, free of charge, respresented his people at the British Boards of Inquiry. Upon his death, he left his large fortune and library to help found the University of Manitoba. His name is still kept alive by the Isbister Building on that campus and in a series of scholarships, the Isbister Awards, which are given annually, by the Mantioba government, for superior academic achievement to students in grade twelve.

What percentage of Métis children received an education is impossible to trace but an early historian stated:

> that quite a number of prairie people, in whose veins French and Scotch blood was mixed with that of the native race, had received a fair education.[11]

By 1810 the Métis were firmly established across the West and South into what was to become United States' territory. Wherever buffalo or furs were to be found, there also were the Métis. Not yet a cohesive group, they needed a catalyst to mould them together. The English-speaking half-breeds were more scattered than the French-speaking ones and their names show a preponderance of Orcadian and Scottish ancestry. Honored names were Henry, Inkster, Isbister, Setter, Harper, Mowat, Omand, Flett, Linklater, Tait, Spence, Ross and Monkman.

More cohesive in spirit, but less settled in residence, were those Métis of French ancestory. The most common names were Boucher, Bois-Bert, Cadotte, Carrière, Chartrand, Delorme, Dumas, Dumont, Flamand, Goulet, Larocque, Lucier, Lagimodière, Morin, Martel, Normand and Villebrun. Isolated as they were, the changes in the French language that were taking place in Quebec did not occur in the West. They kept to old forms but incorporated Cree and English words, so that slowly a different language began to develop. It was composed of obsolete French and a unique vocaulary developed on the prairies; for instance: *aller cri*, to fetch; *fieur*, flour; *patate*, potato; *mouiller*, to rain; *brailler*, to weep; *moucher*, to beat; *fourcher*, to branch off; *charette*, cart; *traine*, sled; *coulée*, ravine or gully; *tetons*, small round peaks; *plateau de coteau*, land system of the river or lake; *babiche*, strip of rawhide; *equipage*, team.

These, then were the Métis people just before the arrival of the first agricultural group, the Selkirk Settlers. A group of people dedicated to a settled agricultural lifestyle would provide the stimulus that would mould these semi-settled Métis into a cohesive group who would, for the next three generations, be a major determinant of the history of Canada.

3

The Years of
Uncertainty

The slow evolution of the Métis people as a nation was interrupted and then speeded up by two events that took place in the early nineteenth century. One was a trade war between powerful rivals, the Hudson's Bay Company and the North West Company, (an association of former free traders in the Northwest) who both sought to control the rich fur trade. The second was closely related to the first and involved the establishment of an agricultural colony of European settlers in the Red River Valley near the forks of the Red and Assiniboine Rivers. In the complex web of intrigue and violence that resulted from these two events, the Métis people were used as pawns and scapegoats by the North West Company. The passions developed in the hearts of Métis people during this period of history hastened their sense of nationhood, developed a sensitivity toward their rights as people who had a stake in the ownership of the Northwest and made them aware of their power when they worked together as a group.

The desire of the aggressive North West Company to gain control of the fur trade was initially manifested on two fronts. On the political front, the Northwest Company attempted to secure a royal charter which would give it a trading monopoly on the Pacific, as well as allow it to ship goods to the Northwest through Hudson Bay. The North West Company was too well established to fear being expelled from the trade in the Northwest for it had opened up the area well in advance of the Hudson's Bay Company. It was, however, hindered by the need to transport goods in and out of the country via Lake Superior and the tortuous river systems. In addition, the rich fur areas so readily accessible via Hudson Bay were too far removed from existing supply depots to be tapped by the North West Company.

Failing to gain a royal charter, the North West Company attempted to buy shares in the rival firm and gain control of the Hudson's Bay Company in this way. As this attempt did not succeed, the North West Company determined to resort to violence. Raids were organized by the Nor'Westers against Hudson's Bay posts; men were assaulted, furs stolen, boats wrecked and loyal Indians threatened. With tensions at an all time high, Lord Selkirk and his Red River settlers entered the history of Rupert's Land. Their entrance was to bring about the last battle in the war for the fur trade and set the stage for a golden age of the Métis.

In Scotland, at this time in history, the clan chiefs owned all the land and the crofters paid heavy rents. As the demand for wool grew, it became profitable to close up the small crofts or farms, and combine them into huge sheep ranches. To this end, farmers were forcibly driven off the lands they had tilled for centuries. Penniless, without food or shelter, those who could emigrated to other countries, while those too poor to pay for passage lived in a state of semi-starvation — indeed many starved to death.

Lord Selkirk, a wealthy Scottish Earl, saw the misery of the displaced families and dedicated his life and fortune to trying to ease the hardships. It seemed to him that the best solution would be to move large numbers of the starving people to a new land where they could quickly become self-supporting through agriculture. The British government gave him grants of land in Prince Edward Island and in what is now the province of Ontario. The settlement in Prince Edward Island proved very successful but the Ontario community of Baldoon on the Detroit frontier was abandoned after the Americans overran it in the war of 1812-14.

As a major shareholder in the Hudson's Bay Company, Selkirk next applied for a grant of land to place a settlement near the Red River. He was granted 116,000 square miles, lying mostly in present day Manitoba but including some of the present province of Saskatchewan and the states of Minnesota and North Dakota. The area was named Assiniboia and the grant was subject to two conditions. Ten percent of the land was reserved for Hudson's Bay men

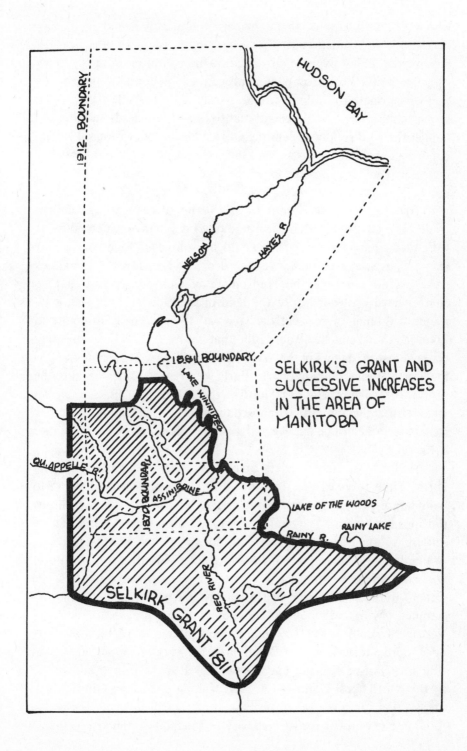

SELKIRK'S GRANT AND
SUCCESSIVE INCREASES
IN THE AREA OF
MANITOBA

HUDSON BAY

1912 BOUNDARY

NELSON R.

HAYES R.

1881 BOUNDARY

LAKE WINNIPEG

QU' APPELLE R.

1870 BOUNDARY

ASSINIBOINE

LAKE OF THE WOODS

RAINY R.

RAINY LAKE

RED RIVER

SELKIRK GRANT 1811

who might wish to settle there and the settlers were forbidden to take part in the fur trade. Selkirk paid ten shillings for the land but was responsible for all expenses incurred in the operation of the colony.

The North West Company opposed the land grant on the grounds that an agricultural colony would disrupt the fur trade. It was reasoned that a colony would be a threat to the buffalo herds and thus endanger the vital supply of pemmican. In addition, the proposed colony cut across the line of communication from Montreal to the West and could, if trouble arose, endanger the trade of the North West Company.

The Hudson's Bay Company saw many advantages. The colony would be a civilized settlement where older company men could retire with their families; the farms would be source of food for the fur trading posts, and the colony, placed on land granted by the Company, would reinforce the Hudson's Bay Company claim that its charter gave it ownership of the land in the Northwest, or Rupert's Land. Although these were the views of the Company directors in London, there can be little doubt that many of the Hudson's Bay trading post managers in the West and North shared the same fears as the North West Company, particularly with regard to the threat to the supply of pemmican. Obviously the Hudson's Bay men in Rupert's Land could not be opposed to the proposed colony, but many were determined to be passive and give the colonists as little assistance as possible.

In 1812, the first settlers arrived at Point Douglas, two miles north of the forks of the Red and Assiniboine Rivers, and began to build houses. In 1813, a new group arrived. In this same year, as in the previous one, there was a shortage of food throughout the area. Those settlers who had arrived in 1812 had, for the winter months, to resort to Pembina, an area approximately one hundred miles south of Point Douglas, where the hunting was better. Even with hired hunters, the settlers were on the verge of starvation that winter and the ensuing summer. Miles Macdonell, the governor appointed by Selkirk, watched his colonists suffer again in the winter of 1813-14, when they once more had to winter at Pembina. Observing the apparently plentiful supply of pemmican that was purchased each summer and stored by the North West Company at their trading post, Fort Gibraltar, in preparation for shipment to posts west and north, the solution to the food problem must have seemed easy to Macdonell. Indeed, he might have felt he had little choice in the decision he was to make. More settlers were expected in the spring and food had to be stockpiled for them if they were to be left free from hunting and able to devote all their time to breaking the soil and planting crops. In January, 1814, Miles Macdonell, governor of the newly formed District of Assiniboia, issued a proclamation which prohibited the export of pemmican, except by license from himself. This was a direct threat to the survival of the outlying fur trade posts, particularly North West Company posts, because it seemed obvious that Macdonell would only give export licenses for any pemmican surplus to the needs of the colonists and the Hudson's Bay Company.

The other aspect of the proclamation, which angered the Métis, was the assumption that a person foreign to the area could enter and suddenly proclaim laws without any regard to the rights and wishes of the people who were native to the land. If Macdonell could do that, what was to prevent him from saying that the Métis didn't own the land they had lived on for generations? It was to the advantage of the North West Company that all the Métis should resent the colonists. This was not easy to achieve, however, for although many of the Métis were associated with the North West Company, some were employees or sons of employees of the Hudson's Bay Company and they were loyal to it. Some action was needed which would draw most of the half-breeds, English and French, together in a common cause.

Miles Macdonell supplied the cause. He came to believe that the Métis system of "running the buffalo" was driving herds out of the District of Assiniboia, so that in July, 1814, he issued a proclamation which forbade the running of buffalo. The Métis people rose up in anger and, subtly encouraged by the North West Company, spoke openly of how Métis people, not Lord Selkirk, owned the land. No one, they claimed, had the right to make laws oppressing the Métis. Were they not a nation of people with rights and privileges second to none? What the Métis needed at this moment was a leader to fuse them into that nation — a New Nation. The man was there, an employee of the North West Company. His name was Cuthbert Grant.

Cuthbert Grant was born in 1793 at Fort Tremblante in what is now Saskatchewan. His Scottish father was a trader for the North West Company, while his mother was Indian, probably Cree, from the Qu'Appelle region. The father died in 1799, when Cuthbert was six

37

years of age, and the boy spent the next several years with his brothers and sisters, in his mother's country. Like many of the White fathers of Métis children, Grant Sr. had directed in his will that his sons be educated. The boy was therefore taken to Montreal in 1801, given some initial instruction and then sent to Scotland to live with his White relatives to receive further education, possibly near his father's Scottish home of Grantown-on-the Spey. (This was the probable origin of the name given to the Métis settlement founded by Grant in later years — Grantown — now known as St. François Xavier.) Nothing more is known of Cuthbert Grant until 1812, when at age nineteen, the North West Company gave him a job as clerk in the Upper Red River District in the Northwest. The year following the arrival of the first settlers in the West and at the height of fur trade rivalry, Cuthbert Grant had returned to Rupert's Land. By 1814, when Macdonell had issued his proclamations, Grant was established in the West and was well known to the Métis people.

Rumors of the troubles in Red River over the export of pemmican would be common knowledge at all points west, for communications between posts were frequent. Macdonell's efforts to control the pemmican supply included a battery of guns set up on the Assiniboine to stop river traffic, as well as an armed attack on a North West Company post at Souris, where he impounded the pemmican supply he found there. With the second proclamation, which forbade the "running of buffalo", and the resulting anger of the Métis who saw their livelihood being taken away, the North West Company began to plan how the Métis might be used to destroy the Red River Settlement. It was decided to assist in creating a New Nation of Métis that would be in opposition to the settlers.

With this in mind, the North West Company appointed Cuthbert Grant as Captain of the Métis and at the same time made officers of other prominent Métis employees. Grant entered into the plan with youthful and understanding enthusiasm. To him the cause of the North West Company and the Métis was one and the same. Later, when he realized that he had been used as a pawn, his loyalty changed. No longer was it divided between the North West Company and the Métis; from that moment, he worked solely for the ideal of a New Nation. Thus he stands at the beginning of the New Nation, as Louis Riel stands at the end.

During the winter of 1814-15, the North West Company tried, with some success, to persuade the colonists to move to Canada where better farming conditions would be found. Subtle threats and promises of better land persuaded many that they would be wise to leave the Red River Settlement as soon as possible and, in the spring, a number did so.

The spring of 1815 found Grant at Fort Gibraltar converting more and more Métis to a belief in a New Nation, in which Métis rights could not be trampled upon by the proclamations of the Governor of Assiniboia, Miles Macdonell. At Red River, Grant and his Métis followers now began a systematic harassment of the colonists who remained. Settlers were fired upon, workmen were chased from the fields, cattle were driven off and stacks of hay set afire. The settlers' fort at Point Douglas was fired upon, although no effort was made to storm the walls.

The North West Company was pleased. As long as the Métis and the settlers fought each other, Miles Macdonell had no time to try to interfere with the passage of pemmican up and down the river. The settlers could not hope to work their land and would soon become discouraged and leave if the Métis persisted in their attacks. In an effort to stop the trouble, Macdonell surrendered to the North West Company and was sent to Canada under arrest.

Peter Fidler, a Hudson's Bay Company employee, and himself the father of a larger Métis family, was temporarily put in charge of the colony. In the negotiations which followed, Fidler was told by the Métis that all colonists must leave and that the Hudson's Bay Company would be allowed to remain only as long as an annual tribute was paid. The new governor hesitated and the Métis attacked the colony again, burning a number of settlers' houses.

Under such pressure, Peter Fidler signed the following treaty with the Métis:

1. All settlers to retire immediately from this river, and no appearance of a colony to remain.
2. Peace and amity to subsist between all parties, traders, Indians, and freemen, in future, throughout these two rivers, and on no account any person to be molested in his lawful pursuits.
3. The honorable Hudson's Bay Company will, as customary, enter this river with, if they think proper, three to four of their former trading boats, and with four to five men per boat as usual.
4. Whatever former disturbance has taken place between both parties, that is to say, the honorable Hudson's Bay Company and the Half-

breeds of the Indian territory, to be totally forgot and not to be re-called by either party.

5. Every person retiring peace-able from this river immediately, shall not be molested in their passage out.

6. No person passing the summer for the Hudson's Bay Company, shall remain in the buildings of the company but shall retire to some other spot, where they will establish for the purpose of trade.

> Cuthbert Grant,
> Bostonais Pangman,
> William Shaw,
> Bonhomme Montour,
> The four chiefs of
> the Half-breeds,
> James Sutherland,
> James White.
>
> Red River Indian Territory, Forks, Red River, 25 June, 1815[1]

All seemed settled. The settlers left for Jack River (Norway House) on the first leg of the journey home. Most of the Métis went to the plains to hunt buffalo and Grant returned to his duties at Qu'Apelle. Grant and his triumphant Métis hoisted, for the first time recorded, a flag of the New Nation.

> "It is red with a figure 8 placed horizontally in the middle of it . . ."[2]

At Red River, however, the colonists had returned under the leadership of Colin Robertson, who was on his way south with a new party of colonists when he met the fleeing settlers by the Jack River, at the north end of Lake Winnipeg. Encouraged by the new contingent of settlers, the colonists enthusiastically began to rebuild their homes and till their lands.

In late fall of 1815, there arrived a new governor for the colony, Robert Semple. Unfortunately, Semple, while touring the District of Assiniboia went to Qu'Appelle and committed a major blunder in demanding that Grant surrender the North West fort with its supplies of pemmican. Grant naturally refused and this imprudent action of the new governor ruled out any possibility of negotiating a peaceful settle-ment of the dispute.

Relations between Semple and Grant having deteriorated, the North West Company kept the kettle boiling by bestowing a new title on Cuthbert Grant.

> "the flag was flying in honor of Cuthbert Grant having been ap-pointed Captain-General of all the Half-Breeds in the country, and likewise rejoicing for the news brought by Swan River MacDonald that the Half-Breeds in Athabasca, English River, Saskatchewan and Swan River were collecting under their several chiefs and sent information that

they would all join Grant early in the spring to sweep Red River of all the English."[3]

In March of 1816, Fort Gibraltar, the North West Company post at Red River, was seized by Governor Semple. The trade route of the North West Company was cut in half, for he who controlled the fort also controlled the passage of boats and canoes on the Red River. In May, pemmican from the Hudson's Bay Company at Qu'Appelle was being transported to the Red River to feed the colonists. Grant, with about seventy Métis, captured it and began to ride towards Red River. On the way they captured Brandon House, a Hudson's Bay Company fort. With boatloads of pemmican travelling on the Assiniboine River, the mounted Métis rode along the banks as guards of the boat brigade. A clash was inevitable as the Nor'Westers and the Métis had the pemmican and were determined to open the river, while the settlers under Semple were equally determined to keep the river blocked and to retain all the pemmican within the District of Assiniboia.

Grant wanted to gain control of both the Assiniboine and the Red Rivers. He controlled the Assiniboine now and hoped to cut across the prairie and get to the Red River north of the settlement without a conflict. In this way, he hoped to cut off the supply route to the settlement and starve out the settlers. On June 19, 1816, he led a group of fifteen Métis across the prairie with pemmican supplies for the proposed camp on Frog Plain north of the settlement. The settlers sighted them and Semple, with twenty-four men, marched out to intercept the Métis at a place known as Seven Oaks. When the two armed parties met, Grant sent a Métis to Semple demanding his surrender. An argument started; Semple seized the reins of the Métis' horse and attempted to disarm the emissary. A shot was fired by a settler and the battle began.[4]

The settlers had no chance, even though they initially outnumbered the Métis, for the sound of gunfire brought a group of fifty more Métis to the scene. Experienced hunters and sharp-shooters, the Métis fired a volley of shots and then fell to the ground to reload. The naive settlers cheered for they thought that their few aimless shots had killed all the Métis. The Métis reloaded their guns and charged the settlers. With the notable exception of two or three, the settlers turned in terror and tried to escape by running to the river and hiding along the bank. The Métis horsemen then charged and shot them with the ease of men accustomed to "running the buffalo". The battle lasted

41

only fifteen minutes. Twenty settlers were killed, while only two of Grant's men died. The Bois Brûlé took out any remaining anger on the corpses by mutilating the bodies. The colony was shattered and on June 22 all colonists left Red River under the personal protection of Cuthbert Grant.

Pierre Falcon, the minstrel of the Métis, who took part in the battle, composed a song[5] which expressed the feelings of the Métis. Titled "The Battle of Seven Oaks", it expresses the pride of the Métis in their new-found military ability.

While the colony at Red River was being quietly abandoned by the settlers, Lord Selkirk was on his way from Montreal with a group of discharged Swiss soldiers (members of the des Meurons regiment who were hired by Britain to fight the Americans in the war of 1812-14). It was his hope that these soldiers would bring peace and order to the District of Assiniboia. Hearing of the crushing defeat of the settlers at Seven Oaks, Selkirk seized the North West Company post of Fort William. An advance group of the des Meurons soldiers reached the Red River in January of 1817 and recaptured Fort Douglas from the North West Company.

Grant, at the head of a group of Métis, returned in March from Qu'Appelle, hoping to recapture Fort Douglas, but did not make the attempt. In June, Grant again came to Red River, this time in a vain attempt to reopen the river in order that pemmican could once again be freely transported. An attempt was made at this time to arrest Grant but the Métis refused to let this happen to their leader. Aware of the new military strength of the colony, Grant voluntarily surrendered and was taken to Lower Canada where a Grand Jury determined there was no cause to try him for the murder of Robert Semple. He was subsequently freed and returned to the Northwest. Later, by proxy, he was tried by the Courts of Upper Canada and again cleared of the indictment. The North West Company laid the blame for Seven Oaks on Grant and, as a result of these experiences, he began to realize that the Company had used him for its own purposes. In future Grant's loyalties would lie with the Métis people and not with a fur company. A personal tragedy entered his life at this point, for when he returned to Qu'Appelle in 1818, he discovered that his wife and infant son had disappeared. Soon afterwards he married again *marriage du pays* (since no clergy were available, the couple simply made a public announcement that they were married) but this marriage proved unsuccessful; in 1820, his wife left him and Grant took his baby daughter to be raised by his sister, Mrs. John Wills.

Meanwhile Selkirk's visit with the des Meurons soldiers had created a new spirit within the colony. Plans were drawn up for roads and bridges; sites were chosen for a school and a church; a treaty was signed with the local Indians, which included Chief Peguis and his recently arrived Saulteaux Indians. The Cree Indians objected to the fact that the Saulteaux Indians were grandly selling land to Selkirk when the Saulteaux were interlopers in the area. Traditionally, for perhaps 1500 years, the Cree and Assiniboine had owned the Red River area. Indeed, one reason Peguis was so helpful to the settlers was to gain allies, for at no time did the Cree or Assiniboine Indians fully accept his intrusion into the valley. It was, however, a sign of the times. The Saulteaux Indians slowly but surely drove the Cree and the Assiniboine out of much of Southern Manitoba and Saskatchewan. The battle was still being waged when the Saulteaux rather arrogantly resold the land to the Canadian government in 1871. In selling the land to Lord Selkirk, Chief Peguis noted that he didn't recognize that the Métis had any claim to the land. It is reported that Bostonnais Pangman, a Métis with a reputation for violence, told chief Peguis that if he continued to talk in such a matter the Métis would settle the argument by killing all the Saulteaux. Apparently, it settled the argument. Such was the violent tenor of the times.

The war between the fur trading companies continued, with the raiding of forts and aggressive competition for the rich fur areas of the Athabaska region. In 1819, the Hudson's Bay Company captured, at Grand Rapids (where the Saskatchewan flows into Lake Winnipeg), the brigade of boats bringing the North West Company's winter fur catch from the Athabaska area. The North West Company retaliated by ambushing and capturing the 1820 fur brigades of the Hudson's Bay Company at the same place. It became apparent to both companies that trade wars helped neither and negotiations to bring about amalgamation took place. In 1821, the two companies combined but continued to use the name of the Hudson's Bay Company. Peace had come again to the Northwest, but the amalgamation of the two companies had a tremendous impact upon the Métis. Almost every rich fur or pemmican area had two posts, one for each company. After amalgamation, only one post was needed in each area and the Hudson's Bay Company had to solve the problem of a surplus of employees. It did so by encouraging people to settle at the now permanent colony at Red River. That the Company directors in London felt a deep sense of responsibility for the surplus employees is shown by an excerpt from a letter sent by them to George Simpson, Governor-in-Chief of the Hudson's Bay Company's Northern Department and dated March 8, 1822:

> We understand that there are an immense number of women and children supported at different Trading Posts, some belonging to men still in the Service, and others who have been left by the Fathers unprotected and a burden on the trade . . . .
> . . . It comes to be a serious consideration how these people are to be disposed of . . .[6]

Simpson then goes on to outline the measures taken so as to ensure that the ex-employees would be well provided for: the establishment of churches and schools; grants of land; assistance with basic necessities, such as clothing, tools, seeds and ammunition; and provision for orphans.

During the years 1821-25, many Métis families were moved to the Red River. If the heads of families had held high rank in either company, they were given extensive land holdings and formed part of the elite of the colony. Indeed, some of the large stone houses they built upon the banks of the Red River, north of the established colony, still add grace and beauty to the Winnipeg area. Alexander Ross, a local historian and also head of a Métis family, had this to say:

> They (the Métis) were not, indeed, united together by the Company's aid into one joint association as buffalo-hunters, which under all circumstances might have been the best plan, yet individually they were taken by the hand the moment they arrived. Those who wished to settle were allowed lands on their own terms; others were taken into the service and employed in every possible way they could be made useful; while such of them as were able hunters received every encouragement, got advances, and were fitted out with everything necessary for the plains, to be paid for at their own convenience.[7]

Many of the Métis refused to move to the Red River colony. Some preferred to move to Pembina, while others formed small villages at various places on the plains. Such villages generally were discouraged by the Hudson's Bay Company, for they were potentially detrimental to trade. Such a settlement developed near Fort Pelly and another at Fort Ellice. The people had large gardens, small grain fields, did some trading and trapping and remained relatively independent. It was at Pembina, however, which was close to the vast buffalo ranges, that the largest numbers of Métis had concentrated over the years.

Peter Fidler, the Hudson's Bay Company surveyor, had declared Pembina to be south of the forty-ninth parallel, the new boundary between the United States and British North America. As such a large concentration of hunters and trappers might contribute to the establishment of an American trading company just south of the border, the Hudson's Bay Company determined to move these Métis to the Red River settlement. In 1823, large numbers of Métis did move from Pembina. To persuade them to move had apparently been quite easy as the Sioux Indians had become hostile and had attacked the settlement several times; in 1822 fourteen Métis had been either killed or wounded. Upon arrival in Red River, they were settled near the Forks and remained there for two years. A large restless group such as this boded ill for the future peace of the colony. Governor Simpson called upon Cuthbert Grant to assist in solving the problem. The idea was born of developing a new community in which the Pembina and other interested half-breeds would be given land. The settlement would meet the needs of the displaced persons from Pembina and also serve as a buffer between the increasingly hostile Sioux and the Red River Settlement.

Accordingly, Grant was given land west of the Red River Settlement on the White Horse Plains by the Assiniboine River, where he settled with approximately fifty families and established Grantown (now St. François Xavier). It was from this settlement that the famous buffalo hunts of the Métis were organized, largely under the leadership of Cuthbert Grant.

During these uncertain years, various churches and schools were also organized amongst the Métis. Although most Métis were nominally Christian, the first clergymen to establish themselves permanently in the Red River Settlement did so only in 1818. Father Provencher and Mr. Edge organized a parish and a school at Red River while Father Dumoulin established a mission and a school at Pembina, where he was later joined by Edge.

In 1818, Provencher wrote to a friend saying:

> Our Bois brulés give us great hope, they are easily taught, they are generally intelligent, and they will learn to read in a short time.

The Roman Catholic priests were determined to educate the Métis and solved the problem of the movement of families from the village of Pembina to follow the buffalo herds by hiring a Mr. Lagasse to live with the hunting party.

> . . . none of these children would otherwise have been able to receive any instruction during the whole winter, since the buffaloes have remained so much farther out this year than usual.[8]

Early in the mission field history, the Roman Catholic Church, for educational and spiritual reasons, set a precedent by following the Métis people as they hunted the buffalo.

In St. Boniface, the school was well established and Provencher, now Bishop, hoped that an exceptionally intelligent half-breed, Victor Chenier, would begin classical studies and become a priest. Apparently in 1825, Victor upset the Bishop by quitting school and going to live with his family at Pembina, where he earned a livelihood as a buffalo hunter. Not even the offer of the teacher's position at Pembina would change Victor's mind.

In 1825, the Nolin sisters, Métis girls from Pembina who had been educated in Quebec, came to St. Boniface and, under the authority of Bishop Provencher, opened a school for girls which was an immediate success.

The Red River Settlers, close to whom were a number of English speaking half-breeds, had more difficulties in providing education for their children. The Hudson's Bay Company brought out Francis Swords in 1812 to be schoolmaster, but found him unsatisfactory and sent him back to England in 1814. The next year, John Matheson became schoolmaster, but that school ended when the attacks of the North West Company took place.

With the arrival of the missionary, Rev. John West, in 1820, Protestant churches were permanently established. A school in the settlement was also established in which, although many of the half-breeds spoke no English and some of the Scots only Gaelic, English was the language of instruction. With the influx of Métis people from the discontinued trading posts throughout the Northwest, a residential school and farm was established for orphans and other children who might be sent by their parents. These two church-controlled schools, plus a number of private schools which sprung up, met the basic educational needs of the area.

The increasing interest in education was encouraged by the Hudson's Bay Company throughout the Northwest. In 1823 the Company passed a regulation that required every father to attend divine service regularly with his family, speak to them only in English or French and teach the children the alphabet and catechism. By 1825, educational opportunities were available, in theory at least, throughout Rupert's Land.

As the first quarter of the nineteenth century ended, the Métis had established themselves as the most influential group in the Northwest. They had adapted some of the technology of Europe to the prairie environment. The buffalo hunt had been established as a commercial venture and Red River carts were opening up the trackless plains, as the canoes and York boats had opened up the waterways. The first major conflict had arisen between the Métis and the incoming European settlers. Although neither side won a decisive victory, a new respect and caution was obvious when Europeans dealt with the Métis. Churches and schools had entered the West and the refining influence of both was becoming apparent. Now most Métis had access to these services rather than just the privileged few, as had been the case in the past. Many at Pembina, St. Boniface and Grantown were becoming farming, as well as hunting people. More and more inter-marriages between Europeans and Indians were taking place as the white male population increased and thus the mixed-blood peoples grew rapidly in numbers. The home of these people would be Rupert's Land, for in all of British North America it was the only place where to be of mixed-blood was to be of the majority group and, therefore, socially acceptable.

It was to be in the Red River Valley that the unique lifestyle of the Métis would develop. It was the training ground for Métis priests, teachers, traders, and even poets. As a hybrid race, they were sturdy, industrious and independent. As in all frontier areas, there were a multiplicity of characters who found ready acceptance in the wide open ways of the West. One of these men became the minstrel of the Métis.

Pierre Falcon, son of a North West Company clerk and a Cree woman, was born in the Swan River area, but was sent to Quebec to be educated. On his return, at age fifteen, he worked as a clerk for the North West Company. With the amalgamation of the two great trading companies in 1821, Pierre, with his wife, a sister of Cuthbert Grant, moved to the Red River Valley and subsequently took up land at Grantown. A dark skinned man with a sparse beard, he wore his hair in Métis style — that is, to the base of his neck. He wrote poetry

47

and composed music for his poems. Every important occurrence was recorded by Falcon in verse and song. His songs were sung by voyageurs on the rivers, cartmen on the trails and by everyone at the frequent social occasions. Many of the major events in the history of the Métis from 1810 to 1875 are recorded in the poems and songs of Pierre Falcon. In his honor, his contemporaries gave the name Falcon Lake to a lake on the border of present day Manitoba.

Many of the European fathers of the Métis were different from the average men of that time. Since they were educated men, in a country of uneducated people, and thus driven to converse intellectually with themselves, perhaps one might expect strange things to happen. No founder of a Métis family made a greater contribution to Canada than did Peter Fidler. Strange though his life may have been, his death brought about a stranger event.

Peter Fidler, an Englishman, born in 1769, became an apprentice with the Hudson's Bay Company at the age of nineteen and worked for the Company until his death at age fifty-three. In his work, he travelled from Hudson's Bay to Peace River and Lake Athabaska, explored and mapped the Saskatchewan and Churchill Rivers and surveyed the land in the Red River settlement. In the process of opening up the country, he built the following trading posts; Chipewyan (1791), Bolsover (1799), Chesterfield (1800) and Nottingham (1802). In addition, he was manager at Brandon House, Swan River Post, Cumberland House, Manitoba House, Fort Dauphin and Norway House. Fidler's Fort, in what is now Winnipeg, was named after him.

Peter married Mary (a Métis or Indian woman) in 1821. The interesting point is that he began living with her in 1794 and had thirteen children before he decided that the union should be made legally permanent. One more child was born after their marriage.

Fidler died at Norway House in 1822 and left behind him a strange will, which is still the basis for much discussion. The will directed that his wife receive a generous and open account at the Hudson's Bay Company, so that she would never want during her life. The interest on his money was to be used to assist his children until they were adults. At that point the interest on the money (a capital of approximately £2000) was to accumulate until 1969, two hundred years after he had been born, and this sum, which would be in the millions of dollars, was to be given to the male heir in direct descent from his youngest son, Peter Fidler.

The administration of the estate was left to three executors; the governor-in-chief of the Hudson's Bay Company, the governor of the Red River colony and the secretary of the Hudson's Bay Company. In 1827, these executors gave over the administration of the estate to the eldest son, Thomas Fidler.

In 1969, it was found impossible to trace the disposition of the monies. Whether Fidler's immediate descendants were able to get the money is unknown. If the records of the unspent portions are ever discovered, the thousands of Métis in Canada with the name of Fidler will doubtless become very interested in history.

Grant, Falcon and Fidler are typical of founders of countless Métis families. They were an educated group in the Northwest and, having the tremendous power and prestige of fur traders, chose a superior type of mate from amongst the Indian women. The hybrid results of such unions combined the knowledge of the Indian and the European. The blending of the two cultures produced a new and vigorous one that, when concentrated in the Red River Settlement, was to generate a strong sense of identity as a new people inhabiting a new nation.

4

The Golden Age
— Part 1

The Battle of Seven Oaks can be considered as the incident that focussed the developing sense of nationalism among the Métis. It was through this episode that the Métis began to see themselves as a unique group in the Northwest. More and more métissage,[1] the inter-marriage within their own group, occurred and this furthered the growing sense of identity. At this time, there also developed the large, superbly organized buffalo hunts. Prior to this, the buffalo hunts had been carried on by a single family or by small groups of families. The ever growing demand for buffalo meat and hides provided the financial incentive for organized hunts which could efficiently harvest the vast herds. To meet the ever growing demand for more buffalo, the Métis penetrated deeply into traditional Sioux territories and, quite naturally, aroused the hostility of the plains tribes. Hunting in large groups afforded the Métis a degree of protection from these warriors of the plains.

Normally there were two major buffalo hunting expeditions each year. The summer expedition usually began in June and sought to bring back sufficient meat and hides to repay the debts that the Métis had accumulated over the winter with the Hudson's Bay Company. In the fall, another expedition set out whose primary purpose was to collect food for use during the coming winter. During the first twenty years of organized hunting, there was a yearly increase in the number of half-breeds participating. In 1820, the hunt was comprised of 540 men, women and children. By 1840, it had increased to 1210. During the hunt of 1846, such large numbers participated it was necessary to organize in two distinct bodies, a group from the White Horse Plains (Grantown) and a Red River section. In 1860, 2,690 Métis took part in the hunt.[2]

The organization of the hunt was done in an open and democratic manner. The men would assemble at an agreed-upon rendezvous (often the Pembina Hills) and elect a governor and ten captains. These men determined the rules of the hunt. Each captain would then pick ten soldiers to assist him in enforcing camp discipline. The governor would read out the rules to a general assembly. Although differing slightly for each expedition, certain rules appeared to form a basic core which were understood and appreciated by all.

1. No buffalo to be run on the Sabbath Day.
2. No party to fork off, lag behind, or go before without permission.
3. No person or party to run buffalo before the general order.
4. Every captain with his men, in turn, to patrol the camp and keep guard.
5. Any person convicted of theft, to be brought to the middle of the camp and the crier to call out his/her name adding the word "Thief" each time.[3]

The rules were strictly enforced, for the need to operate as a cohesive and well desciplined group at all times was imperative for two reasons: the orderly harvesting of the buffalo and protection in case of attack by the Sioux. The rules were rigid, as were the penalties for breaking them. For a first offence, the offender's saddle and bridle were cut up. For a second offence, the offender was brought to the center of the camp, where his coat was cut off his back. The punishment for the third offence was the most severe and humiliating. The offender would be brought before the ten captains who, acting as a military court, would decide whether the offender would be fined, flogged or banished.

Some of the most stirring exploits of the Métis were associated with the buffalo hunt. Their constant battles with the Sioux Indians provided many exciting tales which were recorded by observers and still persist in the oral history of Métis today. In 1851, a crucial and decisive battle was fought, which climaxed generations of fighting and established the Métis as undisputed masters of the plains.

The background of this Sioux-Métis battle is rooted in the native ancestry of the Métis. Traditionally, the Sioux were rivals of the Cree and Saulteaux Indians. The Cree and Saulteaux had slowly driven the

Sioux out of the plains in what is presently Manitoba and Saskatchewan. A "No-man's Land" formed between the rival groups. The Métis, usually a product of the marriage of a White man to either a Cree or Saulteaux woman, thus became a rival of the Sioux. In commercializing the harvesting of buffalo, the Métis invaded traditional Sioux hunting grounds. The basis for the continuing enmity was the question of control of the grazing lands and thus of the buffalo.

The 1851 summer expedition was comprised of three Métis parties who rendezvoused at Pembina. They were the St. François Xavier party of Cuthbert Grant, the Pembina Party and the St. Boniface Party, which was accompanied by a new priest, Father Lacombe who was to prove to be a dedicated friend to the Métis for many years to come. In all, the parties numbered 318 hunters and 982 women and children. There were 1,100 carts with several thousand horses. The grand council met at Pembina and decided to search for the herds as three separate groups, but, for security reasons, to remain in a parallel position with a distance of twenty to thirty miles between each group.

On July 12, the St. François Xavier party led by Pierre Falcon, and composed of 67 hunters, 200 carts and an unknown number of women and children, decided to set up camp in the vicinity of the Grand Coteau. The scouts who had been surveying the area brought back news of a Sioux camp nearby. Five scouts were sent out to study the Sioux camp in detail. Having estimated the general size of the encampment, the Métis horsemen decided to move closer to gain more detailed information. They were sighted and soon surrounded by a band of warriors. Two of the Métis escaped and returned to warn the camp. They were pursued by some Indians who attempted, without success, to gain entry to the Métis camp under the guise of a peace parley. The Métis had decided, as a protective measure, never to allow any Indians into the camp, for fear that the information gained would weaken their defensive position in case of an attack by the enemy.

The Métis prepared the camp for combat. The carts were placed in a circle with wheels touching one another and the shafts tilted up and outwards. Within this barricade was placed the livestock, while women and children crouched under the carts in pits that were dug to shelter them from arrows and bullets. The men dug rifle pits outside the circular encampment at a distance which ensured safety for the animals and families within the circle of carts.

While these defensive measures were being taken, a scout had been sent to the other Métis hunting parties with a request for help. Unknown to the Métis, the scout was captured and killed by Sioux scouts. The morning of July 13 saw the Métis surrounding their priest, Father Laflèche, who celebrated Mass and distributed the sacrament to "all who desired to die well". As the religious observances were ending, the scouts signalled that the Sioux were coming. The Métis were shocked by what they saw. A mass of plumed warriors which seemed to be the whole of the Sioux nation was silhouetted against the horizon. There were between 2,000 and 2,500 Sioux. When the Sioux arrogantly demanded that the small body of sixty-seven Métis turn the camp over to them, the Métis realized that the large numbers of Sioux warriors gave the Indians an arrogance and assurance that boded ill for the half-breed camp. Indeed the task of defence appeared hopeless. The best the Métis could hope to do was die valiantly.

The first Sioux advance met with temporary defeat, as the Indians could not withstand the accurate shooting of the Métis buffalo guns. Inside the camp, Father Laflèche, wearing a white surplice and with crucifix in hand, encouraged the men and soothed the women and children. In the midst of the attack he mounted a cart and exhorted God to give victory to the Métis. It was a comforting sight for the Métis but, no doubt, disconcerted the Sioux.

As the Indians withdrew in discouragement, one of the captured Métis scouts, Malaterre, attempted to escape his captors. He was brought down by a barrage of arrows and bullets. The Sioux then mutilated the body and waved the remnants at the Métis. Rather than terrifying the half-breeds, it shocked them and they became more determined to sell their lives dearly.

The second Sioux assault was carried out in the typical Indian fighting manner. They encircled the camp and used the traditional method of sniping here and there, making sudden dashes individually or in small groups, rather than as a unified body. The Sioux, however, were easier targets than the Métis, who were protected in their rifle pits. Sioux casualties began to mount while the Métis remained untouched. Thus the second Sioux advance failed as had the first one.

Upon withdrawing to reorganize themselves, the Indians were overcome with shame to think that thousands of them could not overwhelm less than one hundred Métis. In anger, they attacked once more en masse but the blistering fire of the Métis toppled warrior after warrior until, thoroughly disheartened, the Indians withdrew. As the Métis cautiously rode out into the empty battlefield, the blood stained grass gave evidence of the large numbers of Indians who had been wounded or killed. They found the body of Malaterre, pierced with three bullets and sixty-seven arrows, and buried him on the prairie.

On July 14, the Métis decided to break camp, though there still remained a possibility that the Sioux would attack again. After less than an hour's ride, the Sioux did attack, but the Métis quickly wheeled their carts into a defensive position and again repulsed the Indians, who suffered large losses once more.

The Indians, having observed the white gowned priest on several occasions, thought the Manitou had given him as a guardian of the Métis and were convinced that his special powers were what gave victory to the half-breeds. Convinced that the Métis could not be defeated the Sioux chief came forward under a flag of truce and swore that never again would his people attack the Métis. The Métis were acknowledged to be the new Masters of the Plains by the bravest warriors in North America.[4]

Skillful as they were on the hunt, many Métis also believed that such skills and virtues came to them through the influence of the priests. The important role played by Father Laflêche at the Grand Coteau indicated the close ties existing between the church and the half-breeds. This association between the Métis and the Roman Catholic Church dated back to 1818 — the year in which Mgr. Provencher established his mission at St. Boniface.

The Roman Catholic missionaries had come to Red River for several reasons.

a) Some of the first Selkirk settlers were Roman Catholic and a priest had been promised them as a condition of settlement.

b) It was thought that missionaries could help restore the peace at Red River after the decisive battle at Seven Oaks.

c) The Hudson's Bay Company believed that missionaries working amongst the half-breeds and Indians would raise the moral standards of the people and ensure a greater degree of social stability.

When Provencher arrived at Red River in 1818 he found that the people had little understanding of the concepts and ideals of Christianity. Their religious tenets were based more on Indian than Christian beliefs. The first reaction of the half-breeds to the priests was one of caution. They tended to look upon Fathers Provencher and Dumoulin as medicine men who could cure the sick. To complicate matters for the priests, many Métis spoke an Indian language, usually Cree, and French and English were secondary languages. The onus was upon the missionaries to either learn the Indian languages or teach French or English to the Métis.

The missionaries followed the Métis to the buffalo hunts, the fur trapping grounds and the fish stations. Even when living with the Métis on the plains, the missionaries attempted to make them aware of the advantages of permanent agricultural settlements. Farming, the priests rightly argued, would supplement the hunt and help banish the periodic suffering from famine which plagued any people living by the hunt. Some Métis were converted to part-time farming, while others retained the hunt as their only source of livelihood. The coming of the Protestant missionaries in 1820, and their subsequent creation of farming communities for half-breed sons of Hudson's Bay men and the local Saulteaux Indians, brought an element of competition to the cause of agriculture development. Those who did try to spend all their time as farmers saw their efforts frequently result in failure. The conversion of the half-breeds, of whatever faith, to the sedentary life of farmers proved to be a greater challenge than converting them to Christianity.

From the writing of the priests come some of the more detailed descriptions of half-breeds during this period of history.

In 1870 Mgr. Taché wrote an account of his impressions of the Métis which he begins with a description of their physical characteristics ("handsome men, large, strong and well made"). He then lists a number of other traits: an instinct peculiarly Indian, their powers of observation, an excellent memory, sense of humor, intelligence and skill as horsemen. In a remarkable list of their virtues and faults, he includes, under the former heading, their warm-heartedness, willingness to help, love for children, patience and honesty ("theft is a crime scarcely, if at all, known amongst Half-breeds"). His list of faults refers to drunkenness, frivolity, a desire for immediate gratification, love of pleasure, generous hospitality, love of freedom, independence and improvidence.

He later makes an interesting reference to the imminent disappearance of the buffalo: "Fully sensible of the fearful crisis through which we must pass when buffalo hunting fails. . ." This remark prefaces a series of comments about the social condition of the Métis in which he compares the French- and English-speaking half-breeds. He concludes his observations with a defence of the Métis vis-a-vis the Battle of Seven Oaks.[5]

From Mgr. Taché's account, it is apparent that a considerable degree of acculturation towards European lifestyles took place between 1816 and 1860. The influence of the church was the primary factor and the social character of the Métis owed much to the Christian missionaries. Many of the old customs continued past the period recorded by Taché and were still observable in Métis communities in 1972. One of these is the custom of "kissing in the New Year". It indicates a religious influence as well as the perseverance of ancient French and Scottish customs introduced into the Northwest in the first part of the nineteenth century. One elderly Métis, when interviewed in 1972, made the following comment:

> My father, continued to follow the custom handed to him by his Dad. It was a custom within Métis families from long ago to the turn of the century to request from the priest, the New Year's blessing. My Grandfather, as head of the family would go forth and obtain it. Upon receiving it, he would then come home and there, starting with his wife and then the children from the eldest to the youngest, he would in turn bless them. Then the New Year's kissing would start. Métis families followed this custom which stems from the French.[6]

The custom continues to this day in many Métis communities.

Another Métis custom, which caused mixed reactions amongst white people and consternation to the clergymen, was that of having dances that might continue for several days. The custom has not changed for one hundred and fifty years, if the oral tradition is correct, for such parties are still common with the Métis.

> "Everyone would assemble at a particular home where all the furniture was removed and piled outside. The chairs and a small table were kept. The table served as the liquor bar and food stand. The only other piece of furniture kept was the stove. In summer this also would be removed. The preliminaries done, the dancing would commence with the men first doing the toe-tapping (jigging). The women would then follow. Since many Métis, who attended such dances were fiddle players, the dancing would often times continue for days on end or at least until liquor, food and energy were all exhausted.[7]

The establishment of Lord Selkirk's settlement of 1812, and the bringing of half-breeds to the Red River following the amalgamation of the fur trading companies, had introduced farming as a viable and alternative lifestyle to hunting. The churches persisted in their efforts to convert the Métis to farming, with varying degrees of success. The English half-breeds apparently were more amenable to a sedentary life than the French. However, the churches received support from the Hudson's Bay Company in their efforts. Governor Simpson had realized early the military potential of the Métis. The marauding Sioux were a constant threat to the Red River Settlement and Simpson decided to ally himself with the churches and solve several problems at once. He wished to protect the Red River settlement, gain some control over the nomadic half-breeds and at the same time draw the people at Pembina to the north, in order to lessen the chances of American trading posts developing just south of the forty-ninth parallel. He determined to grant a large area of land to Cuthbert Grant, a Scottish half-breed, who had become leader of a large number of French half-breeds. The land granted was to develop into a center where the Métis could become farmers and which would also serve as a buffer zone between the Settlement and the Sioux.

Grantown was situated approximately eighteen miles west of the confluence of the Assiniboine and the Red Rivers. The boundaries to the South and West bordered the traditional hunting grounds of the Sioux. The site of the settlement was ideal since the land was fertile and, most important, was traversed by the Assiniboine River and had a plentiful supply of wood needed for houses, fuel and the construction of carts.

Cuthbert Grant designed the settlement in such a manner that the Métis could be rallied with ease for defensive purposes. His house was situated in the heart of the settlement. It was to this central point that the scouts would report any Sioux marauders and from there the Métis horsemen would launch an attack.

Some one hundred families had settled at Grantown by 1825. The importance of the settlement went beyond that of defense. As a permanent settlement, it soon became a model for other Métis people in terms of the value of developing small farms. If they were not out on a buffalo hunt, the Métis worked the land and cared for domestic livestock. The farms were not intended, however, to be the primary means of subsistence. The farms provided permanent homes, the people were grouped to allow churches and schools to serve them, while the land supplemented the earnings from the buffalo hunts. Although considered a secondary source of food, during poor hunting seasons the farms averted famine. Sometimes, because of the dedication to the hunt as the primary means of subsistence, the farms often went unharvested if the hunt took the men too far afield. Harvesting took place only when the hunt had been completed.

New Métis communities began to develop along the banks of rivers and streams. St. Vital, St. Norbert, Ste. Agathe, and St. Adolphe grew up along the Red. Ste. Anne and Lorette were established on the banks of the Seine River. St. Paul, St. Charles and Grantown were established along the Assiniboine. The English-speaking half-breeds extended their settlements along the Red River to the north of the Fork as far as Selkirk and west of Grantown to High Bluff and Portage la Prairie.

With the development of agriculture, the question of land, law and order, and laws governing trade other than furs became necessary. The Selkirk Settlers' attempt at farming had been totally disastrous during their first fifteen years of practice. Droughts, grasshopper plagues and floods had devastated the area. In order to survive, all men had to turn to the buffalo as a source of food. A dependency upon the buffalo hunt and the fur trade was developed even amongst those whose primary objective was to farm. As more land was cultivated, grist mills were built to convert the grain to flour. The surplus was freighted to far distant fur trading posts to supplement the diet of meat. Paralleling the growth of agriculture, came a need for new items such as harness, ploughs, rakes, scythes, and a multitude of other goods. Where the Settlement had once been a self-supporting enclave with a need for no producer or buyer other than the Hudson's Bay Company, new needs began to develop.

The people in the settlement were economically dominated by the Hudson's Bay Company and its monopoly effectively kept any opposition out of the Northwest. Local merchants did develop, but they bought from the Company, traded with the people, and then resold the goods to the Company. The desire to sell surplus farm produce and furs in the more competitive American market grew. In 1823, local people had opened up small stores, warehouses, etc., and were thus in the "buying and selling" business. Such competition did not worry the Hudson's Bay Company, which had a legal monopoly on buying and selling within the area, so long as local traders acted as sub-agents for the Bay. However, the local merchants soon discovered that they could buy more cheaply in the United States and began to do so. To control these businessmen, the Company passed laws restricting the products that local merchants could buy and sell. Protests were sent to Selkirk's executors who, in turn, protested to the Hudson's Bay Company in London, England and the restrictions were withdrawn. However, to ensure its control, the Hudson's Bay Company increased its freight rates on goods coming through the Hudson's Bay and set a twenty percent duty (later removed) on merchandise imported from the United States. By means of such measures, the Company continued to control trade in the Settlement.

This situation remained stable until 1836, when the Company bought back the land it had granted Lord Selkirk. It then began to dispose of the land by granting acreages to its retired servants, the Métis, churches, and other people who came to the Settlement. However, such lots were not sold nor was a title or deed given in many cases. The land was only leased to the person in accordance with certain conditions. These were:

1. The person to establish himself on the lot within forty days,
2. Remain on the lot and cultivate ⅙ of the land area given him within six years,
3. Contribute to the expenses of maintaining public services (i.e. church, schools, repair of roads, etc.),
4. Refrain from selling furs, leather and alcohol to anyone but the Company,
5. Promise to ship any merchandise through the Hudson's Bay Company; pay five percent of custom on all merchandise plus pay for freight,
6. Promise to maintain peace and order in the settlement and to not do any buying and selling without Company permission, and
7. Lessee could not rent the land to any other person.[8]

The Company was like a feudal landowner in medieval Europe. The only difference was that the Hudson's Bay Company was not bound to provide any services to its tenants.

The restrictions on trading caused great problems for the Métis. By 1835, American trading posts had been established in the Dakotas. Since the buffalo hunts carried the Métis across the international boundary, it was often most convenient to trade with the Americans. The Hudson's Bay Company termed this illegal trade. At this time, in an effort to increase profits, the Company reduced and fixed the price of furs. The Company also threatened the Métis, by reminding them that the land on which they lived could be taken away from them if they continued to trade illegally.

The Métis rose in anger at the Company's actions, which they considered to be unreasonable, and demanded that:
1. the price of produce be raised,
2. facilities for exporting products be provided, and
3. no import duty on United States goods be levied.

The Company answered these demands, and showed its authority, by imposing a seven and one half percent levy on all goods coming from the United States. The Métis argued that they had opened the route to the south and that it was because of their skills and abilities that buffalo hides and pemmican were coming into the Settlement. In return, the Company offered to compromise by lowering its levy to four percent; the Métis once again accepted the traditional authority of the fur trading company.

Nevertheless, the Company attempted to enforce its modified laws by ordering severe punishments for thefts. The Hudson's Bay Company defined theft to mean any illegal trading within the territories under the Company's jurisdiction. Some traders were used as examples as in 1836, when Louis St. Denis was publicly flogged for such trading. So intense were the feelings of the Métis that the local police guard had to be called to protect the man who had administered the punishment.

Severe as the punishments were, illicit trading continued to flourish. Since the Americans could offer goods in trade much more cheaply than the Hudson's Bay Company, many of the Métis resisted passively by squatting on Company land and trading with the Americans as they pleased. So many took this approach that the Company did not bother trying to evict them. So futile were the Company's attempts to enforce its 1835 laws, that by 1840, they were rescinded.

By 1840, Métis trade depended heavily upon the American posts. This meant that the Hudson's Bay Company profits were substantially reduced. In an effort to regain control of trade, the Company, in 1844, began to censor mail. Letters of goods to be imported were opened for inspection by the Company. The importer had to declare that he did not traffic in furs and if anyone were caught trafficking in furs, his land deed, plus all other company benefits, were declared void. Once again the Company used its monopolistic powers, as the only provider of mail services, to exert control over citizens of the Northwest.

The Métis responded with a petition to the Council of Assiniboia asking for a share in the government and also demanding a definition of their special status as natives of the Red River settlement.

Red River Settlement,
August 29th, 1845.

Sir, — Having at this moment a very strong belief that we, as natives of this country, and as half-breeds, having the right to hunt furs in the Hudson's Bay Company's territories whenever we think proper, and again sell those furs to the highest bidder; likewise having a doubt that natives of this country can be prevented from trading and trafficking with one another; we would wish to have your opinion on the subject, least we should commit ourselves by doing anything in opposition, either to the laws of England, or the honorable company's privileges, and, therefore, lay before you, as Governor of Red River Settlement, a few queries, which we beg you will answer in course.

1. Has a half-breed, a settler, the right to hunt furs in this country?
2. Has a native of this country (not an Indian) a right to hunt furs?
3. If a half-breed has the right to hunt furs, can he hire other half-breeds for the purpose of hunting furs?
4. Can a half-breed sell his furs to any person he pleases?
5. Is a half-breed obliged to sell his furs to the Hudson's Bay Company at whatever the price the company may think proper to give him?
6. Can a half-breed receive any furs as a present from an Indian, a relative of his?
7. Can a half-breed hire any of his Indian relatives to hunt furs for him?
8. Can a half-breed trade furs from another half-breed, in or out of the settlement?
9. Can a half-breed trade furs from an Indian in or out of the settlement?
10. With regard to trading, or hunting furs, have the half-breeds, or natives of European origin, any rights or privileges over other Europeans?
11. A settler having purchased land from Lord Selkirk, or even from the Hudson's Bay Company, without any conditions attached to them, or without having signed and bond, deed, or instrument whatever whereby he might have willed away his right to trade furs, can he be prevented from trading furs in the settlement with settlers, or even out of the settlement?
12. Are the limits of the settlement defined by the municipal law, Selkirk grant, or Indian sale?
13. If a person cannot trade furs, either in or out of the settlement, can he purchase them for his own and family use, and in what quantity?
14. Having never seen any official statements, nor known, but by report, that the Hudson's Bay Company has peculiar privileges over British subjects, natives, and half-breeds, resident in the settlement, we would wish to know what those privileges are, and the penalties attached to the infringement of the same?

We remain your humble servants,

JAMES SINCLAIR,	WILLIAM BIRD,
BAPTIST LA ROQUE,	PETER GAROCH,
THOMAS LOGAN,	HENRY COOK,
JOHN DEASE,	JOHN SPENCE,

ALEXIS GAULAT,	JOHN ANDERSON,
LOUIS LETENDRE dit BATOCHE,	THOMAS MCDERMOT,
WILLIAM MCMILLAN,	ADALL TROTTIER,
ANTOINE MORRAN,	CHARLES HOLE,
BAT. WILKIE,	JOSEPH MONKMAN,
JOHN VINCENT,	BAPTIST FARMAN

To ALEXANDER CHRISTIE, Esq.,
Governor of Red River Settlement.[8]

In reply the Council of Assiniboia stated that the Métis had no rights other than those enjoyed by any British subject. This reply had been anticipated, for, although the Red River Settlement (during this period of time known as the District of Assiniboia) had its own governor and council, these were appointed by the Hudson's Bay Company. Typical of the authoritarian and monopolistic approach of the Company was the license to trade issued on July 10, 1845, to a Settlement man.

Fort Garry, July 10th, 1845.
On behalf of the Hudson's Bay Company, I hereby license A. B. to trade, and also ratify his having traded in English goods, within the limits of the Red River Settlement. This ratification and this license to be null and void, from the beginning, in the event of his hereafter trafficking in furs, or generally, of his usurping any whatever of all the privileges of the Hudson's Bay Company.

Alexander Christie, Esq.,
Governor of the Red River Settlement.[9]

The unrest developing among the Métis caused the British Government, at the request of the Hudson's Bay Company, to send an Imperial regiment to the Settlement, which imposed martial law from 1846 to 1849. There is a certain amount of debate as to the basic reason for the stationing of a military force in the Settlement. It has been argued that the Imperial regiment was sent, not to control the Métis, but rather to be ready in case of war with the United States over a boundary dispute between Oregon and British Columbia. Nevertheless, upon removal of the regiment in 1849, a clash occurred between the Métis and the Hudson's Bay Company. The result of this historic confrontation broke the Hudson's Bay Company's fur trading monopoly in the Northwest.

It had become apparent to the Company that some Métis traders had continued an illegal trade in furs. The Company, attempting a show of strength, had three traders, including a Guillaume Sayer, arrested. In this way, the Company hoped to show the people of Red

River that its trading monopoly must be respected. During the trial of the first offender, Guillaume Sayer, armed Métis surrounded the courthouse, ready to take action if the penalty should be too severe. It was apparent to the magistrate and jurors that the peace of the Settlement was at stake. Although Sayer was found guilty, the jury recommended that no penalty or punishment be meted out to him and the magistrate wisely imposed none. The other Métis were never tried. The result of the whole affair was that the Métis, along with other fur traders, interpreted the verdict to mean that " 'le commerce est libre — the fur trade is free". The Hudson's Bay Company could no longer regulate the trade in furs and the trade route to St. Paul, Minnesota, was now open to all.

The man who had organized the show of armed force and brought the news of the non-penalty to his fellow Métis was Louis Riel, Sr., the owner of the prosperous grist mill which had earned him the title of "Miller of the Seine".

Born at Isle a la Crosse, Saskatchewan in 1817 and educated at Berthier, Quebec, where he had studied for the priesthood, Riel had come back to the Northwest in 1843 to join his fellow Métis in earning a livelihood by the buffalo hunt. He married Julie Lagimodière, daughter of Marie Anne Gaboury, the first white woman to reside permanently in the Northwest. Riel and his wife settled in what is now St. Vital, where Riel operated his flour mill and attempted to establish a woolen mill. Since such business ventures were frowned upon by the monopolistic Hudson's Bay Company, his woolen business failed. Because of this, Louis Riel, Sr. became active in striving to break the Company monopoly on business and government in the Settlement.

The freeing of trade following the Sayer trial brought a burst of economic activity and a period of prosperity to the Settlement. The booming economy attracted many settlers and businessmen from Canada and the United States. The infusion of new men with different ideas was to act upon the Settlement as a leaven. Change was in the air but the Métis were unprepared to accept rapid change. In the latter part of their Golden Age, the lives of the Métis people in the Northwest were to be fraught with doubts and uncertainties.

BÉRARD

5

The Golden Age
— Part 2

With their victory at the Sayer Trial, the Métis had been able to close off the first half of the nineteenth century on a happy note. The Hudson's Bay Company fur trade monopoly had been broken and the Métis found themselves able to trade freely on both sides of the border.

However, events were taking place south of the border that were to have a great influence upon the Northwest. One was the concept of Manifest Destiny, a phrase used to describe the desire of Americans to gain control of all of North America. An examination of the geographical importance of the Red River Settlement in 1850 makes clear why the American idea of continental ownership had such an effect upon the history of the Métis.

The Red River Settlement was the heart of the North American Continent and was the administrative center for the fur trade which extended across the prairies and the sub-arctic. The location was of strategic importance as a central point from which troops could control the area. As early as 1846, the Americans had considered the Red River Settlement as a possible area of annexation, for whoever controlled it could control the entire Northwest area.

The boundary line between Canada and the United States had been established in 1818 as the forty-ninth parallel. Despite the boundary line, the ties of Red River with the United States grew stronger each year, for the Métis traded extensively with merchants south of the border. Immigrants from the east, coming to Red River, had to take the train to St. Paul, Minnesota and then come to Red River by cart or boat. By the 1850's, St. Paul had become the major stop over before heading for Red River. A direct line of communication had developed that linked Red River with the United States.

Canadians, especially those from Ontario, were concerned about the growing American influence in the Northwest. *The Globe*, an influential Toronto newspaper, expressed a desire that Western Canada should become settled as quickly as possible, in order to offset the American influence. The Métis, however, gave little thought to either Canadian or American influences, nor did they consider the ways in which these might affect their future. It is perhaps because of this lack of concern about the future that the Métis soon found themselves in a position that eventually led to an insurrection.

Though they had won their court case in 1849, the Métis were quite content to allow the Hudson's Bay Company to rule. Canada West (Ontario) questioned the validity and feasibility of having a commerical organization such as the Hudson's Bay Company control such a vast area of land. It was argued that the company was a hindrance to the agricultural development of the West. Demands were made to have the company monopoly revoked and a new form of government established. Because the company had allowed, in 1836, for the crown to take over if it saw fit, the Ontario newspapers demanded that the Company's license to operate be revoked.

Since the year 1859 marked the end of the Company's license to trade, a British Parliamentary Committee was set up in 1857 to review the issues surrounding the Company's activities. However, the major reason for the committee meetings was to decide whether or not the Northwest was suitable for agriculture, as well as to consider economic activities that might be possible in addition to the fur trade.

Governor Simpson of the Hudson's Bay Company tried to convince the Committee all of Rupert's Land was unfit for agriculture. His arguments were to no avail. The Committee recommended that the Company continue to operate in the northern regions, that lands in the area of the Red and Saskatchewan river valleys be opened for settlement and that Canada should make immediate plans to take over control of the Northwest.

To gain more precise information, the Committee then sent out an exploring expedition under the guidance of S. J. Dawson and H. Hind. The Dawson and Hind expedition conducted studies for the Canadian Government, while the geographer, John Palliser, headed a similar expedition which was charged by the British Government with assessing the agricultural possibilities of the Northwest.

The expeditions came West in 1857-1858 to conduct their investigations. Both parties used Red River as their headquarters and, while there, recorded the obvious fact that all roads lead to the Settlement. They realized that the Red River Settlement must be linked by road with the East and that from it would radiate transportation routes to all parts of the Northwest. The major factors to be considered were whether or not the climate and land were suitable for agriculture.

Both expeditions submitted reports to their respective governments after their explorations. Dawson and Hind claimed that the Northwest must be connected to Canada by a system of land and water communications. By this, the expedition obviously meant the establishment of a railroad. Palliser did not agree. He questioned the feasibility of building a railroad through the muskeg country around Lake of the Woods. Though the findings of these expeditions had indicated that the West could be settled, the reports did not offer any great encouragement. They both implied that agriculture would have to remain an experiment within the west until some future time. Palliser favored a colony extending from the Red River to the Rocky Mountains of British Columbia. This area covered 240,000 square miles. He had found three types of soil within the area and cautioned that the third type should not be farmed. They were:

1. Arable prairie around the Red River.

2. Willow prairie — an area of land which had once been forested but had burned through prairie fire.

3. True prairie — characteristic of the American desert.

Meanwhile, events at Red River had forced the settlement into a state of "partnership for survival" amongst the Métis, the White settlers and the Company. Floods had once again devastated the area and, in 1851, the year of the great flood, the settlement was without any crops. The buffalo had moved away to the western prairies and famine appeared to be imminent. These conditions forced all groups to work for the betterment of the Settlement, in the hope of maintaining its survival. By 1857, the dependence upon one another had switched from one of co-operation to that of open and competitive trade.

The arrival of the Palliser and Dawson-Hind expeditions created a minor worry within the Settlement. People wondered what the effects on such expeditions would be. Was the Hudson's Bay Company giving up the title to the area? Were the people to be consulted or given information concerning these matters? The explorers were hired by and responsible to their respective governments and, as such, were not able to answer the questions posed by the residents of Red River.

To the explorers, especially Dawson, the Red River area appeared most attractive for further settlement.

> . . . the settlement commences about ten miles below Lake Winnipeg, and extends south for some fifty miles along the Red River, and to the westward for about seventy miles on the Assiniboine, there being however, a long interval on the latter river, between the White Horse Plains and the Prairie Portage that is without settlers.[1]

Dawson goes on to state:

> . . . that the settlement should have advanced but slowly is not to be wondered at, considering how far removed it is from the civilized world, but there has been progress, and that of a most pleasing and satisfactory description and I question if at this moment it would not compare favorable with any rural settlement of equal extent in Canada.[2]

In describing the Métis, Dawson suggests that they have adopted the habits of civilized life:

> . . . as they live at present they generally grow enough for their own use and they are possessed of cattle, sheep and horses which demand some measure of attention; but they have also their hunting season.[3]

In his description of the Settlement's institutions, Dawson noted that there were two libraries, nine churches and eighteen schools. He recorded that four of the schools instructed the females of the settlement and that five of the churches were Episcopalian.

Referring to the social conditions of the Settlement, Dawson recorded that crime was scarcely known and that few of the Métis people used indelicate expressions. An indication perhaps, of the major influence of the missionaries. This, then was the picture of Red River that Dawson transmitted to the people of Canada. It was indeed a pretty scene — one that would surely invite settlers. While Dawson was busy with his reports, the Settlement at Red River began to feel the pressures of encroaching civilization.

At St. Paul, a group of merchants had constructed a steamboat which would operate between Red River and St. Paul. In 1859, the *Anson Northup* was launched, and arrived at Red River in May. The new mode of transportation would prove disastrous for many of the

Métis, for a steamboat could carry a heavier and more varied cargo than the cart brigades. Soon the Red River carts were being replaced by steamboats. At the same time the economic value of the fur trade began to decline and a period of slight economic depression became apparent, the brunt of which was borne by the Métis.

In 1859, another outside influence appeared in the settlement in the form of a printing press. Two Canadians, W. Buckingham and W. Coldwell, started a local newspaper called the *Nor'Wester*. Its *raison d'être* was to create agitation in the West for annexation with Canada. To achieve this, the editors, former writers for the *Globe* newspaper in Toronto, demanded that Hudson's Bay Company rule be terminated.

Meanwhile, events on the West Coast, particularly the California Gold Rush of 1849, had created a sudden flow of immigration to the western United States. The frontier there was filling up. The old American dream of annexing Red River was once again actively discussed. Furthermore, because of the gold rush and rapid opening of the American Frontier, many people from the Settlement moved to the United States and became citizens and also fervent annexationists. To complicate local matters, American traders appeared at Red River in considerable numbers. This situation created concern amongst the authorities of the Hudson's Bay Company. Because of the agitation at Red River against Company rule it was feared that the free traders would not only entice the Métis and Indians to sell their furs to the Americans but also secure their allegiance to the powerful republic to the south.

Caught in all this were the Métis. They could foresee dimly that the arrival of steamships and mass immigration meant an end to their freighting business. The buffalo moved deeper onto the prairies as settlements sprang up in the West. The traditional Métis lifestyle seemed to be slowly coming to an end.

Land had replaced buffalo as the major economic base. It was through the ownership and development of land that the settlement at Red River would expand. But the concept of individual land ownership was only partly understood by the Métis. Had they not lived on it from time immemorial? Did they not own it through aboriginal rights? How could land be more important that the fur trade and the buffalo? Somehow the Métis could not see the broad implications of the shifting economic base. It seemed obvious to them that the buffalo were the only possible source of economic stability.

Meanwhile agitation continued in the hope of making Canada realize the importance of annexing Red River. Theories of government were expounded. It was obvious that, should the Imperial Government in London, England, decide to suspend the Company's license to trade, there would have to be a change in government at Red River. Three forms were discussed as possible solutions. The Imperial Government could establish a crown colony controlled by Great Britain. Second, there was talk of joining Canada. Third, talk centered around the possibility of joining the United States. The latter appeared to be most appropriate, since Red River had closer ties with St. Paul's than with Ottawa. In reality, Red River was isolated from Ottawa. But demands by the Canadians for annexation of the Settlement to Canada continued to grow. Petitions and complaints were sent to the Imperial Government in England, but the government would do nothing. The Hudson's Bay Company was still the sole ruler of the area and its title must first be relinquished before the Imperial Government could take over. Canada herself had not yet been established as a country. She would have to create her own union before the Imperial Government would even think of transferring the land to it.

Coldwell and Buckingham continued to attack the Company rule through their newspaper. They wanted union with Canada, as did the English Métis leader, James Ross, who later bought the newspaper. Ross demanded self government for the Settlement as a first step. Support for his cause grew as Dr. John Christian Schultz joined with him. Along with their followers, they formed the Canadian Party, a political group whose main objective was to unite the Settlement with Canada. In 1865, Schultz bought out Ross's newspaper and used it as a political vehicle to attack the Council of Assiniboia and the Hudson's Bay Company, and to urge the extinction of Indian title to the land. Schultz was, in fact, attacking the traditional basis of the Settlement. The Canadian Party correctly made the point that the Company was not meeting the new social and economic needs of the people in the Settlement. During the period from 1864 to 1867, every group in Red River apparently wanted to change the form of government, but a consensus could not be reached.

Natural occurrences then began to make matters worse within the Settlement. From 1862 to 1868, the Settlement went through a period of drought. Grasshoppers also plagued the area. At the same time the crops failed, as did the hunting and fishing. Red River had become too dependent upon these sources of produce and sank into another economic depression.

By 1869, a road has been started from Lake of the Woods to Red River. Known as the Dawson Road, it cut through Hudson's Bay Company territory and the lands settled by many Métis. Thus an actual take-over of certain land seemed, to the Métis, to have been launched by the Canadian government.

In the talks that were going on in London about the possible transfer of Hudson's Bay Company lands to Canada, not one Métis representative was involved. The discussions were to result in the end of Company rule in Rupert's Land and the beginning of a resistance by the Métis people in order to protect their rights.

6

The Insurrection

The immediate causes of the Red River Insurrection are numerous, but there was one basic reason for the Métis unrest which is ascribed to by the majority of historians. Dr. G. F. G. Stanley, author of *The Birth of Western Canada* and *Louis Riel*, perhaps explained it best when he described the confrontation as one of civilization facing the frontier. The Métis people were interested in the survival of their way of life and feared progress. They wished to be left alone to live their own lives in a world set apart. Because the Métis attempted to halt the inevitable encroachment of civilization, the Red River Insurrection was doomed to fail.

During the 1850's and 1860's, the settlement at Red River was largely isolated from Canada. Its major communications were through Hudson Bay or from Minnesota in the United States. Consequently, there was no strong bond connecting the area called Canada and the people called Canadians with the Settlement, except for a few of the recent immigrants.

Geographically, the Northwest had closer ties with the south, for it was separated from Canada by hundreds of miles of almost impossible terrain, while the placid Red River connected the Settlement with the United States. The trade of the Settlement was transported either by way of Hudson Bay to the North or St. Paul in the United States. The government was provided by the Hudson's Bay Company. The Scottish settlers in the area had come from the British Isles. As a result, the Red River settlement developed stronger ties with both the United States and Britain than with Canada.

ring this period, when the young Louis Riel was a student at
ège de Montreal, more Canadians arrived in the settlement and
egan to urge the union of the Northwest with Canada. Dr. Schultz, a
medical practitioner turned businessman, became the acknowledged
leader of this vociferous group and *The Nor'Wester* served as the
voice of the pro-Canada people. They attempted to gain support by
criticizing the rule of the Hudson's Bay Company and advocating confederation with Canada. However, the ties of trade, communication,
and, in many cases, personal and family relations, were factors binding the Settlement to the United States. The agricultural potential of
the Northwest made it desirable territory and it was considered a prize
to be sought in the expansionist designs of the United States (especially Minnesota). John A. Macdonald and his government were aware of
the American desires. This issue in itself caused great concern to Macdonald and his government, for hopes of a Dominion from sea to sea,
as stated in the British North America Act, would be destroyed if
Canada were unable to gain control of the Northwest Territories.

So as to forestall the American Annexationists, an agreement
was hastily negotiated in 1868 with the Hudson's Bay Company, the
terms of which were that the Company would dispose of its rights in
the Northwest to Canada for a token cash payment of £ three hundred thousand. Although the agreement had not yet come into effect,
in August, 1869, the Minister of Public Works for the Canadian
Government, William McDougall, sent John Stoughton Dennis and a
crew to begin surveying the Red River Settlement. Dennis and his surveyors were to be the spark that ignited the flame of resistance within
the Métis.

Conditions in the settlement — drought, grasshopper plagues
and, on occasion, famine — pointed increasingly to the need for a
change. More importantly, perhaps, the poor economic conditions
created a mood of discontent in the minds of many people in the
Northwest. An unhappy people can easily be driven to extremes by
slight misunderstandings and one arose with the coming of Dennis.

Colonel Dennis arrived at the Red River Settlement on October
4, 1869. On October 11, Louis Riel, Baptiste Tourand and a group of
Métis prevented Dennis and his crew from surveying the hay privilege
(hay fields behind the farms lining the river). When asked to explain
this action, Riel explained that the Canadian Government "had no

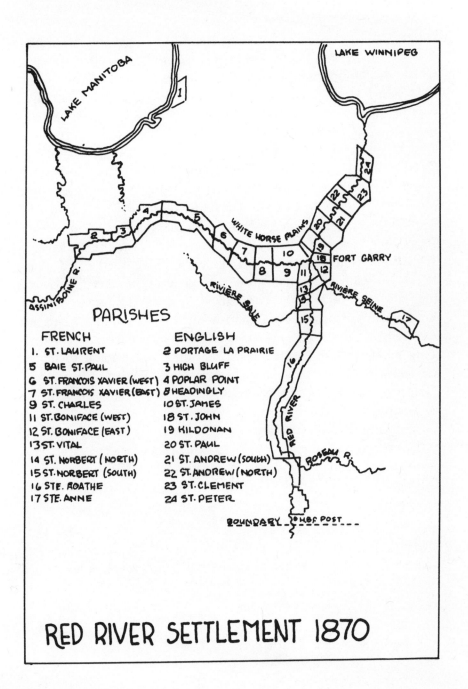

LAKE WINNIPEG

LAKE MANITOBA

LAKE MANITOBA

1

24

23

22

21

20

19

WHITE HORSE PLAINS

FORT GARRY

4

3

8

5

6

7

10

8

9

11

12

13

14

15

17

RIVIÈRE SALE

RIVIÈRE SEINE

ASSINIBOINE R.

16

RED RIVER

ROSEAU R.

PARISHES

FRENCH
1. ST. LAURENT
5. BAIE ST. PAUL
6. ST. FRANÇOIS XAVIER (WEST)
7. ST. FRANÇOIS XAVIER (EAST)
9. ST. CHARLES
11. ST. BONIFACE (WEST)
12. ST. BONIFACE (EAST)
13. ST. VITAL
14. ST. NORBERT (NORTH)
15. ST. NORBERT (SOUTH)
16. STE. AOATHE
17. STE. ANNE

ENGLISH
2. PORTAGE LA PRAIRIE
3. HIGH BLUFF
4. POPLAR POINT
8. HEADINGLY
10. ST. JAMES
18. ST. JOHN
19. KILDONAN
20. ST. PAUL
21. ST. ANDREW (SOUTH)
22. ST. ANDREW (NORTH)
23. ST. CLEMENT
24. ST. PETER

BOUNDARY ___ HBF POST ___

RED RIVER SETTLEMENT 1870

right to make surveys on the territory without express permission of the people of the Settlement."[1]

The Métis turned to Louis Riel for assistance with their difficulties. To seek leadership from Riel would seem natural to the Métis. As the best educated man in the area, he had both an understanding of politics (gained through his friendships in Quebec) and a knowledge of law garnered while working in a law office in Montreal. In addition to this, Riel had the language skills necessary to be a leader in the multi-cultural Northwest. He could speak French, English, and Cree fluently. These skills, together with the respect earned for the Riel name by his father at the time of the Sayer trial, combined to give him considerable stature in the eyes of the Métis.

At this time, William McDougall, the soon to be appointed Lieutenant-Governor of Red River, was on his way to the Settlement. McDougall, Colonel Dennis and Charles Mair[2] were associated either directly or indirectly with the Canadian party and became the focus of the animosity of the Métis. There were many voyageurs, buffalo hunters and cartmen in Red River who depended on the fur trade and the Hudson's Bay Company for a livelihood. They were an independent group who were ready to fight, rather than submit to forced change and what they considered to be foreign control. All that was needed was a leader and Louis Riel was the man who emerged to fill that role.

A National Committee was organized to resist the Canadians. John Bruce, a kindly man, but one who lacked leadership ability, became the President, while Louis Riel, the real leader, was elected Secretary. Riel, Abbé Ritchot, Abbé Dugas and the National Committee met at St. Norbert and drew up the following message to the approaching Governor McDougall:[3]

> Monsieur:
> Le Comité National des Métis de la Rivière Rouge intime à Monsieur McDougall l'ordre de ne pas entrer sur le Territorie des Nord-Ouest sans une permission spéciale de ce comité.
>
> Par ordre du président.
John Bruce
Louis Riel, Secrétair
>
> Daté a St. Norbert, Rivière Rouge
> ce 21e jour d'octobre, 1869

The prevention of McDougall's entry into the Settlement was effected for two reasons: to prevent McDougall and the Canadian par-

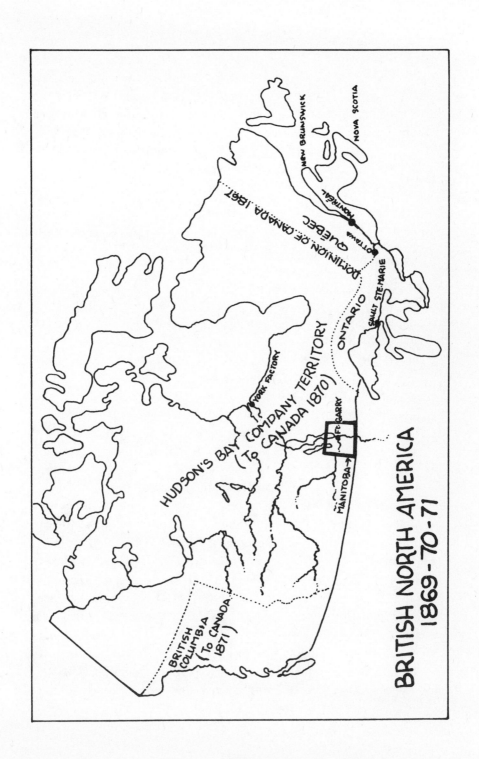

BRITISH NORTH AMERICA
1869-70-71

NOVA SCOTIA

NEW BRUNSWICK

MONTREAL

OTTAWA

QUEBEC

DOMINION OF CANADA 1867

SAULT STE-MARIE

ONTARIO

YORK FACTORY

HUDSON'S BAY COMPANY TERRITORY
(To CANADA 1870)

Ft. GARRY

MANITOBA

BRITISH COLUMBIA
(To CANADA 1871)

ty from seizing power and to delay the transfer of the Northwest to Canada until the Métis could negotiate reasonable terms.

The Métis and White settlers had not been consulted and their fear of change and of foreign domination caused them to resist. The traditional land and language rights appeared to be in jeopardy and their chief desire was for a legal guarantee of such rights. The Métis fear of a Canadian take-over and of then being placed under the authority of such hated men as Dr. Schultz and Charles Mair caused the strongest reaction. Such a government would be intolerable to a group of people who, as Kreutzweiser says:

> . . . had been accustomed to a wild and free life. The situation with regard to them, when analyzed, is seen to be that of a wild and un-trampled ethos.[4]

A way of life was threatened, and for the buffalo hunters at least, increased settlement would destroy their livelihood. It was natural for a freedom loving people, so threatened, to resist what they believed to be external domination.

Governor McDougall had arrived at Pembina when he received the note from the Métis National Committee. He proceeded to the Hudson's Bay Company post just across the 49th parallel, where he was halted by an armed group of half-breeds and then escorted back to Pembina and ordered to remain there. On the same day, Riel occupied Fort Garry. By November 1, his adherents had increased to four hundred men who had taken an oath of allegiance. The provisions stored in the Fort were necessary for the maintenance of this large group. Riel also realized that the control of the Fort, the center of the Settlement, allowed him to dominate the entire area. There was little opposition to this move, for the Hudson's Bay Company had neither troops nor the time to organize a protective force. The Governor of Assiniboia, McTavish, was seriously ill and Dr. Cowan, the second-in-command, could offer only verbal objections. A stalemate had been reached. The Métis controlled the Settlement and McDougall was confined to Pembina. McDougall would have been wiser to have returned to Ottawa, for he was without military force, but his obstinant nature would not allow him to retreat. By remaining, he may have hoped to foment a civil war. Such a course of action would have met with little success, however, for Riel was securely in control.

Riel had issued a proclamation calling for a council to be established which would be composed of twelve English-speaking and twelve French-speaking members. Riel was shrewd enough to realize that success in making a strong impression upon Ottawa depended upon gaining the support of the English half-breeds and White settlers. When the convention met to elect the Council there were fiery exchanges between Riel and those who urged the Red River Settlement to join the United States. A proclamation from Governor McTavish citing the unlawful basis of the insurrection and urging the convention to disperse was put to good use by Riel. It rallied the Métis to Riel's side for they realized that only by united action could their goals be accomplished. The convention adjourned, but reconvened on November 23. The same arguments continued, however, and that same day, Riel decided to replace the old Council of Assiniboia with a Provisional Government. The people of the settlement were still loyal to the Queen, but, with Riel's proposal, the English moderates joined with their French-speaking neighbors.

During this time, the Canadians were intent upon frustrating Riel's plans. They encouraged McDougall to remain in Pembina until the West had become part of Canada. On December 1, McDougall issued a proclamation appointing himself Lieutenant-Governor of Rupert's Land. To the proclamation he forged the name of the Queen. Perhaps McDougall did not realize that the transfer that was to have gone into effect on December 1 had been postponed by Macdonald because of the insurrection and therefore McDougall was not officially Lieutenant-Governor. Even if he did not know it, there seems to be no excuse for his forging of official documents. It seems clear that McDougall was bent on conquest from the beginning, when he sent Colonel Dennis to Red River and when he, as a Lieutenant-Governor, arrived in Pembina with a supply of three hundred rifles. The forging of the proclamation, however, is indicative of both the frustration and desperation felt by McDougall. The forged documents fooled no one, for Riel was relatively sure that the proclamation was not legitimate. The proclamation was read to the convention, which met again in December, but no one took it seriously. The convention delegates drew up a list of Rights, but broke up when they could not reach agreement on whether McDougall should be allowed to enter the Settlement if he guaranteed the List of Rights. Those Canadians present had succeeded in stalling the work of the convention, but their success was to be momentary. When an attempt failed to have Colonel Dennis organize a military force from among the few Canadians who had armed themselves, Schultz and forty-eight Canadians were forced to surrender to the Métis. The principal Canadian leaders were forced to surrender to the Métis and thus ended up in Fort Garry as prisoners. McDougall returned to Ottawa in despair and, on December 10, the flag of the Provisional Government of Red River flew above Fort Garry. On December 27, John Bruce resigned and Louis Riel was elected President.

Riel was not, however, completely secure in his position. He had failed to construct a wide and solid foundation for his government. He still had the loyal support of the French-speaking half-breeds, but the English-speaking half-breeds still wavered. The English-speaking delegates had dispersed, and now Riel and his lieutenants, a "rump" of the convention, formed a virtual dictatorship. As funds were scarce, Riel was forced to find money for a considerable number of men had to be maintained as a military force. From Governor McTavish he demanded £1000 which was refused. Riel then had the Company's safe opened by force, taking the £1,090 found in it; two days later, John Bruce seized goods worth £3,000 to supply the Métis military forces. A receipt for the money and an itemized list of the goods taken were deposited with the Hudson's Bay Company. The legality of the action is a point which many historians debate. Some claim that it indicates that Riel and his Métis followers were common thieves. The incident is used by some in an attempt to prove that Riel was nothing more than a power-seeking criminal who used unethical means to attain his goal. The Canadian Government later paid the debts incurred with the Hudson's Bay Company by Riel and his men.

Until the Provisional Government was proclaimed, disinterest in the affairs of Red River was manifested by the Canadian Government. In December, however, Macdonald dispatched two emmisaries to Red River: Victor Thibault, a French-Canadian priest, and Colonel de Salaberry, a French-Canadian soldier. Macdonald and his cabinet did not understand the grievances of the Métis. They saw the insurrection as an expression of French-Canadian parochialism and hoped that the two French-Canadian commissioners would be able to placate the Métis and half-breeds. The Ottawa delegates, however, had no authority to promise anything, and under such circumstances, serious negotiations proved impossible. In any event, Thibault soon came to sympathize with the Métis cause and refused to be a party to attempts to coerce the people of Red River.

The Canadian Government next appointed Donald A. Smith, later Lord Strathcona, to negotiate with the people of Red River. He was a man of experience and knowledge who, as the husband of a Red River half-breed and the manager of the Montreal branch of the Hudson's Bay Company, had considerable knowledge of the situation. When Smith arrived, he prudently left his official papers in Pembina, and was non-commital when Riel attempted to find out what concessions he was authorized to grant the Métis. Smith had, in fact, received more authority than the previous delegation, and this, coupled with his superior diplomatic skill, caused Riel to realize that Smith was a man to fear. Smith was successful in bribing some of the more prominent Métis leaders (he was alleged to have spent £500) and proceeded to out-manoeuvre Riel. Smith agreed to send a friend to Pembina to get his official papers, whereupon Riel ordered the arrest of the messenger. A group of Métis intercepted the man returning with Smith's papers, and despite Riel's request that the papers be given to the Provisional Government, the Métis guards, for some unknown reason, conveyed both papers and messenger to Smith. Riel was forced to negotiate with Smith, who refused to reveal the contents of the papers and his commission from Ottawa except at a public meeting of the entire settlement. Riel could do nothing but comply.

On January 19, a public meeting was held in an open field in the settlement and was attended by people from the scattered villages along the Red and Assiniboine Rivers. One thousand men and women waited in below zero weather to hear Donald Smith present the case for Canada. Smith's commission was simply to convey to the people the intention of Ottawa to respect their rights and to allow them to exercise such control over their settlement as was consistent with British tradition. The people stood for five hours on that cold January day to listen to the debate. It was to be Donald Smith's day of victory. By the time the meeting was ended, there were cries of "Free the prisoners!" Riel's authority appeared to be in jeopardy.

On the second day of the meeting, however, in the presence of an even larger crowd, Riel emerged as the real victor. Father Lestanc, Thibault and de Salaberry had been using their influence to sway the crowd. Smith had made his point, however, and good feelings prevailed in the Settlement. Riel's recommendation that Mr. Smith's commission be considered at a new convention was approved unanimously. It was obvious that there was almost whole hearted support for the drawing up of a more complete List of Rights; the only dissenters were the Canadians.

On January 26, the newly-elected convention delegates met at Fort Garry and over a period of several days drew up a detailed "List of Rights." The demands were moderate:

1. An elected legislature
2. Representation in the Canadian Parliament
3. Appropriation of public lands for the building of roads, schools, etc.
4. Official status for both French and English languages in the courts and legislatures
5. Winnipeg to be connected by rail with the nearest railway
6. Steam communication between Lake Superior and Red River within five years
7. The franchise be granted every man over twenty-one
8. The confirmation of all existing "privileges, customs and usages".*

*(This extremely vague statement was to be variously interpreted in the future.)

Having approved the List of Rights, the Convention formally elected a new Provisional Government representative of all the Red River Settlement. Louis Riel was chosen President and ordered by the Convention to release all prisoners. This was done immediately. In addition, the Provisional Government chose delegates to travel to Canada to negotiate for entrance into confederation on the basis of the List of Rights. On February 10, the Settlement celebrated in anticipation of a return to peace and quiet.

But this mood of calmness and satisfaction was to be short-lived, for the Canadian party was still dissatisfied. One Thomas Scott, with several others, had earlier escaped confinement in Fort Garry on January 9, prior to the general release of all prisoners, and fled to safety in the Portage la Prairie area. Schultz also escaped and a band of Canadians assembled at Portage and marched on Fort Garry, with the intention of freeing the rest of the prisoners. On arriving in Winnipeg, however, they found little sympathy and less assistance for their cause. Dispirited, they were returning to Portage la Prairie when, in passing by Fort Garry, they were sighted by the Métis sentries. Believing they were about to attack the Fort, the Métis soldiers intercepted and captured them. In an effort to safeguard the peace by a show of power, Riel threatened to execute Major Boulton, the reluctant commander of the Canadians, but was dissuaded from doing so by Donald A. Smith. One of the prisoners was Thomas Scott, who, on February 18, found himself once again in the jail from which he had recently escaped. A strong Orangeman (an organization which was violently anti-Catholic) and a loyal Canadian, Scott was an unruly prisoner. He was disdainful of half-breeds and apparently delighted in openly criticizing and insulting them. The Métis had little patience with Scott and, on one occasion, when several of the guards were preparing to give him a severe beating, only the personal intervention of Riel saved him. It is apparent that, if ever there was a hated Canadian prisoner, it was Scott. His insults and threats of bloody reprisals became unbearable and a court martial was set up. Scott was charged with insubordination and disloyalty and was found guilty. On March 4, despite the appeals for clemency by Reverend Young, the Methodist pastor, Riel allowed the sentence of the court to be carried out. Thomas Scott was executed by a firing squad.

No action of Riel's has caused so much criticism and speculation. His reason for allowing the execution to take place can only be guessed at. Some maintain that it was compulsive vengeance. Others contend that it was either because of pressure by the Métis — in particular the guards — or a deliberate act of policy. The Orangeman believed there was no doubt as to the motive. They believed Riel sought to show his authority as President and that he personally ordered Scott to be shot and then buried in an unmarked grave. A favorite sentence of the Orangeman was "Scott was in very truth shot down like a dog, and like a dog was buried." In fact, the sentence and execution reflected the rough and ready, but traditional justice meted out to recalcitrants on a buffalo hunt.

Up to this point, the insurrection had been relatively quiet. There had been, with the exception of Scott's execution, no bloodshed. Riel justified Scott's execution by claiming that the Orangemen were, in fact, making war against the Settlement and the Provisional Government. Although the consequences of the execution must have been realized, it appeared that Riel never made any overt attempts to stop it. Surely Riel's power was such that he did not have to yield to the wishes of a few guards? Perhaps the most reasonable explanation is that, for Riel, Scott had become a symbol (as both Riel and Scott later became in Eastern Canada) of all that Riel despised; of all the bigotry and hatred that he had fought against. It is reasonable to assume that Riel was infuriated by Scott's officious, insulting and disdainful attitude towards the half-breeds and, in a moment of fury, allowed the execution to occur. This single action would drive Riel into lonely exile and be the determining factor in the government's decision to hang him in a later decade.

The Canadians, the Scots and the moderate half-breeds were horrified by the execution. The shooting was a blunder — an unnecessary blunder. With the solid support of an elected government behind him, Riel could have released Scott and laughed at his insults. After the Scott execution, the peace of Red River remained unbroken, but it was an uneasy peace. The faith of Riel's supporters was shaken and the imminent negotiations with Canada were jeopardized. There was no further attempt to overthrow Riel, nor was there any serious opposition to the Provisional Government, but he had lost some of the confidence and faith which the people had given him before the execution.

The reaction in Ontario was far more serious, however. Scott's origins were Ulster-Irish and, long before coming to Red River, he had been a loyal Orangeman, a member of a body which postulated the superiority of an Anglo-Saxon heritage and was violently opposed to Roman Catholicism. Fiery speeches, protest rallies and stories of Métis cruelty were used by members of the Orange Order to stir up the populace of Eastern Canada, particularly in Ontario, in the hope of forcing the government to avenge the execution of Scott. The government's position was precarious, however. The anti-French and anti-Catholic protests in Ontario caused an opposite reaction in Quebec. The Conservative party, which was then in power, could not afford to alienate either province, since an election was to be held in the near future. The government's alleged promise of an amnesty for the "rebels" only added fuel to the fire which already was burning hotly in Ontario.

On March 22, shortly after Scott's execution three delegates from the Provisional Government, Abbé Ritchot, Judge John Black and Alfred H. Scott, representing the French-speaking, the English-speaking, and the American interests respectively, were dispatched to Ottawa. They had negotiating powers only; final ratification of any agreement was to be made by the Provisional Government. Black and Scott were largely ineffective in Ottawa, but Abbé Ritchot rigorously applied himself to the difficult task at hand. By continued application, questioning and argument, Ritchot was able to persuade the Conservative Party to put the Manitoba Act through the House. When passed, it contained most of the demands in the List of Rights, with a special section asserting the land rights of the half-breeds and guarantees of the continuation of a bilingual school system.

Ritchot also pressed for an amnesty for the leaders of the insurrection. However, because Red River was still a British Colony, the granting of it had to come from the Queen. He received a verbal assurance that the Canadian Government would apply for one. What he did not know was that with the application for amnesty the Governor-General sent a note stating that it was not the desire of a united Canadian Cabinet. In addition, there was forwarded a petition from the Orange Order stating that the amnesty would be unjust if it included the leaders of the insurrection. During this time, Bishop Taché worked behind the scenes trying to ensure that an amnesty would be granted. All efforts in this regard failed, for the Canadian Government was caught between two equal and opposing political forces; Ontario and Quebec. John A. Macdonald did what he had to do to gain his party the most votes: he compromised. He expelled Louis Riel from Canada for a period of five years. It was not until 1875 that an amnesty was given to the leaders of the Red River Insurrection.

With the passage of the Manitoba Bill, A. G. Archibald was appointed Lieutenant-Governor. To aid in the setting up of the new Manitoba Government and to restore stability to the Red River Settlement, a military force was dispatched to the west under Sir Garnet Wolseley. One of the promises given Bishop Taché by Macdonald had been that a civil government would be established prior to the arrival of the peace-keeping force. This was not the case, however, for the force arrived on August 25, considerably ahead of Archibald. The Canadian government had also avowed the peacefulness of Wolseley's mission but, after three months marching through the wilderness, the cry of the soldiers was for the lynching of Riel. Riel was forewarned of the hostility of the troops, however, and, when they arrived, there was only an empty fort to greet the invading soldiers. Louis Riel had fled. As he departed Riel said,

> No matter what happens now, the rights of the Métis are assured by the Manitoba Act; that is what I wanted — my mission is finished.[5]

The Red River Insurrection had ended. The Provisional Government of Riel had not existed in vain, for it had forced the hand of Canada. Differences concerning the transfer of the territory from the

Hudson's Bay Company to Canada had been reconciled. The Métis had agreed to accept union with Canada and their actions had precipitated the establishment of the province of Manitoba in 1870. The Canadian Government was forced to negotiate with the people of the Red River Settlement, a policy which, if initiated earlier, would have avoided the need for an insurrection on the part of the half-breeds.

Louis Riel was the product of a local situation, but became a national symbol of Canada's eternal problem of racial and religious strife. His government cannot be termed a rebel government, since there was no legal government against which to rebel. The Hudson's Bay Company had signed away its authority and Canada had not yet taken responsibility for hers. Technically, Riel's government was legal, as it filled a vacuum.

The insurrection was the expression of a group of people, frightened by the thought of change and wary of an unknown outside force. It was, in the main, democratic, an expression of self-determination arising out of a desire to retain traditional rights and freedoms.

One may condemn Riel, the man, for his mistakes and his personal, intellectual and emotional weaknesses. Riel, as an individual, pales to insignificance before the desire for freedom inherent in the Métis people. The Red River Insurrection, was, in many ways, an effort to halt the encroachment of an advancing agriculturally oriented way of life. It was also an expression of fear of an inevitable change in their traditional form of local government. They had not been consulted during the negotiations for the transfer of the Northwest from the Hudson's Bay Company to Canada nor had they been consulted about the form of government to be granted them upon union with Canada.

As free men, they were unwilling to have a foreign form of life and government imposed upon them. The Red River Insurrection was the first of a series of efforts by the Métis to protect their culture and their identity against the encroachment of a dominant white civilization. To modern Canadians, Riel is rarely thought of as a rebel or murderer, but rather as a misguided man whose glory rests upon a brief episode in history. To the Métis, the people whom he loved and who fully returned that love, he remains the Father of Manitoba, the

88

voice and the symbol of his people as they fought for their rights as free men of the Northwest.[6]

7

The First Dispersion
Of the Métis

The tension-ridden situation resulting in the formation of Manitoba came at a time in history when several other changes intruded upon the traditional lifestyle of the Métis. The most significant, perhaps, was the transfer of power from the Hudson's Bay Company to Canada. Despite the friction which had been so apparent between the Métis and the Company over several generations, there did exist a working relationship based upon understanding and respect, which had evolved over two centuries. No matter what conflicts arose between the Métis and the Hudson's Bay Company, the relationships between the leaders in terms of economics, blood and personal ties always modified the situation. The Métis were children of the fur trade and, when the political power of the parent disappeared in 1869, unfamiliar and impersonal political bodies were dealt with by the half-breeds in an awkward manner, for they had little understanding of the new social and political structures.

The changes taking place in modes of transportation slowly eroded the economic position held by the Metis as freighters. When the boat, *Anson Northup,* steamed into Fort Garry in 1859, the boom of her whistle signalled the beginning of the end for the creaking cart brigades. The new steam technology soon achieved supremacy over the Red River cart in settlements that had navigable waters. Within three decades, the historic cart disappeared, even on the land-locked transportation routes.

The depletion of the buffalo close to Red River and the migration of the remnants to the far off plains, were other indicators of change that affected the Métis. Because of the need to travel vast distances to find buffalo, it became almost impossible to combine buffalo hunting with part-time farming. A choice had to be made. Population pressures were taking an excessive toll of other wild life and many Métis turned to fishing as a main source of food. In areas such as St. Laurent and Grand Marais in Manitoba, the change from buffalo hunting and farming had been made to fishing and farming and fishing and trapping respectively.

The most profound change after 1869-70 was the social humiliation of the Métis. The victorious Canadians were openly contemptuous of anyone "papist" or "French" or a "breed". As all Métis had at least one of these disadvantages, and all suffered from being visible members of a defeated and despised group, the new province of Manitoba was a hotbed of animosity. As residents of an area that was being inundated with Canadians, who brought new lifestyles and power structures, the "Red River People", Métis and White, suffered. But none suffered like the half-breeds and, in particular, the French half-breeds. The major cause of their suffering was the Canadian soldiers.

The soldiers, released from the tension of an expected battle and a long, hard trip to the Red River, broke loose. The town was filled with drunken soldiers bent on revenge and no person of native ancestry was safe on the streets. Women, especially, were insulted and maltreated. By setting up a strong body of military police, Colonel Wolseley was able to gain reasonable control over the soldiers but, in the absence of martial law, the army leaders had no control over the citizens. Canadians — anti-Catholic, anti-French, and anti-Métis — roamed the streets and a deliberate persecution of the Métis took place. Canadians wanted revenge for the death of Thomas Scott and their animosity was naturally directed towards the half-breeds. The English-speaking half-breeds were largely outside Winnipeg, on their farms north of the village at the Forks, so that the brunt of the persecution was borne by those in the villages of Fort Garry, St. Boniface and St. Vital. Lieutenant-Governor Archibald, in a confidential letter to Sir John A. Macdonald wrote:

92

> Unfortunately there is a frightful spirit of bigotry among a small but noisy section of our people. The main body of the people have no such feeling — they would only be too happy to return to the original state of good neighbourhood with each other; but it is otherwise with the people I speak of, who really talk and seem to feel as if the French half-breeds should be wiped off the face of the globe.[1]

The "small but noisy section of our people" referred to the Canadians.

Threats, brawls, beatings and even death was the daily fare of the persecuted Métis. François Guilmette, the man who had had the unpleasant task of firing the shot that put an end to Thomas Scott, was killed by unidentified persons. Thomas Spence, who had been editor of the *New Nation* newspaper, was beaten savagely. Father Kavanaugh barely escaped assassination for daring to speak out and denounce the persecution carried on by the Canadians. James Tanner was killed when the horses he was driving were frightened and ran away when unknown persons hurled objects at them. André Nault was beaten and left for dead. Bob O'Lone was killed by Canadians in a brawl. Louis Riel, of course, was constantly sought but was carefully hidden and guarded by the Métis.

It was a particularly vicious incident that forced the Métis to make a decision about their future. On September 13, Elzéar Goulet, a member of the court martial that condemned Thomas Scott, was walking on the muddy roads of Winnipeg when he was recognized and pointed out to some soldiers. They, joined by several citizens, tried to capture him. Goulet ran to the river and attempted to swim across it to seek safety in St. Boniface. The pursuers threw rocks at him until one struck its mark and the unfortunate man sank beneath the waters. The body was recovered the next day and buried. Subsequently, an investigation was undertaken by two magistrates, who managed to discover the identity of the murderers. As in all the other cases, the authorities considered it unwise to proceed with prosecution of the criminals, for fear of creating still greater unrest.

A group of Métis held a secret meeting in St. Norbert to discuss the situation. After much discussion a petition was drawn up to be sent to the President of the United States. President Grant was asked to intercede with the Queen on behalf of the persecuted Métis. O'Donoghue, Riel's lieutenant, wanted to ask the United States to invade and take over the Northwest. Riel, supported by the majority,

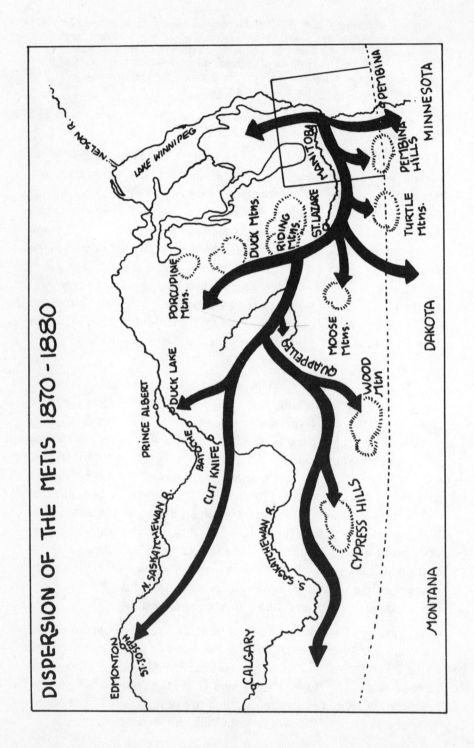

DISPERSION OF THE METIS 1870-1880

NELSON R.

LAKE WINNIPEG

MANITOBA

PEMBINA

MINNESOTA

PEMBINA HILLS

TURTLE Mtns.

PORCUPINE Mtns.

DUCK Mtns.

RIDING Mtns.

ST. LAZARE

MOOSE Mtns.

QUAPPELLE

WOOD Mtn

DAKOTA

PRINCE ALBERT

DUCK LAKE

BATOCHE

CUT KNIFE

N. SASKATCHEWAN R.

S. SASKATCHEWAN R.

CYPRESS HILLS

EDMONTON

ST. JOSEPH

CALGARY

MONTANA

felt that justice could be gained by remaining within Canada and working through the political system.

The decision had been made by the leaders and the average Métis had two choices: remain in the new province of Manitoba or move. They could go either to the United States or west into the unorganized territories. The half-breeds, naturally enough, were not of one mind. A minority left for the United States. A substantial number chose to remain on their farms or establish new farms on the land grants promised the Métis. A large number of the English-speaking half-breeds made this choice. An unknown number of Métis chose to leave Manitoba and attempted to recreate the Red River lifestyle in settlements farther west.

The census of 1870 had shown that the new province of Manitoba (a small district of 11,000 square miles) contained 11,963 persons: 5,-757 French half-breeds, 4,083 English half-breeds, and 1,565 people who classified themselves as White. It was from the 9,840 mixed-bloods that the great trek west was to draw its numbers. From the far-flung trading posts of the West, their ancestors had been drawn to Red River in 1821-25 by the Hudson's Bay Company. Through hunting, trading and freighting with carts, the ties had been maintained and the Métis turned to the vast, but familiar, spaces of the West to seek sanctuary.

For some decades, a slow migratory movement had been draining a few Métis each year from the Red River Valley. Some of the settlements they formed were not too distant — for example, St. Laurent, on Lake Manitoba, and Grand Marais, on Lake Winnipeg. A few people from St. François Xavier (Grantown) and Baie St. Paul had moved to Fort Ellice to join the Métis already there. The small group at St. Lazare slowly added to its numbers. These are typical of many pockets of semi-permanent settlements throughout the West. History, however, rarely recorded details of them, unless either a church mission or a trading post was located in the settlements.

Butler, in a report on the Northwest in 1871, mentioned six major settlements in existence: Prince Albert, White Fish Lake and Victoria were populated mainly by English Métis, while St. Albert, Lac la Biche and Lac Ste. Anne were settlements of French Métis,. Fort Qu'Appelle, Fort Pelly, Touchwood Hills, Cumberland House, Fort à la Corne, Fort Carleton, Fort Pitt and Fort Edmonton had small numbers of half-breeds near them. Duck Lake had been slowly developing as a Métis winter settlement, but was usually deserted each summer, as families went to hunt buffalo. There were, then, small settlements throughout the Northwest, free of persecution and without Canadian rules and regulations, where the old life of the Métis could be continued. It was to these havens that many Métis from Manitoba began to drift. It was a drift rather than a planned exodus. Families left singly or in two and threes, rarely in groups larger than ten or twenty. With all their material goods piled in Red River carts, families would set out and, living off the land, would drift westwards until their destination was reached. Those lacking a specific destination would establish homes in wooded valleys, where fertile land was found and which would serve as a permanent base from which hunting, trapping and fishing could be carried on in the surrounding countryside.

Although migration was slow at first, the problems associated with the Manitoba Act kept the exodus moving steadily for a decade. Section 31 of the Manitoba Act stated:

> . . . it is expedient, towards the extinguishment of the Indian Title to the lands in the Province, to appropriate a portion of . . . ungranted lands, to the extent of one million four hundred thousand acres thereof, for the benefit of the families of the half-breed residents.

It is significant that the Government of Canada, in the Manitoba Act, recognized and settled the rights of the half-breeds to the land before they bothered to negotiate a treaty with the Indians. It would seem that this was more a political than a reasoned legal decision and, perhaps, reflected the relative weakness, both in numbers and power, of the few Indians within the boundaries of the new province.

Rather than solving the land question for the Métis and establishing positive feelings toward the new government, the half-breed land grant did just the opposite. It proved to be a source of irritation which has persisted to the present day.

Certain townships were set aside or reserved for Métis settlement. Not until 1873 did the government begin to allot the land. At that point, the Canadian government, in an example of prime idiocy, decided that adults and heads of families were not eligible — only the children who could prove residence in Manitoba at the time of transfer of Rupert's Land to Canada on July 15th, 1870 were to receive land, at the rate of one hundred ninety acres per capita.

In 1874, the rules were changed and the heads of family were to be given land also, to the extent of one hundred sixty acres or a money scrip to the value of $160 per adult. As many children were absent on buffalo hunts on July 15, 1870, a new census of the Métis was to be taken. This showed 5,088 persons eligible for land but admittedly incomplete — especially as the census of 1870 had registered 9,840 mixed-bloods. The government decided that the newly revised grants would be two hundred forty acres per person and all previous allotments were cancelled in order to start again under the new regulation. By 1879, all the land apparently had been allocated but Métis were still coming off the plains and out of the trapping areas to register.

Confusion reigned supreme.[2] One year a Métis had land, but the next year it was taken away for redistribution. White immigration was pouring into the province and often, when a Métis went to claim the land granted to him, he would discover an immigrant family firmly in possession. Most half-breeds despaired of ever getting their land and sold the paper rights to speculators for a few dollars. Convinced that they would never secure justice concerning land, many didn't even bother to claim it, but simply moved west.

Typical of the disregard of the rights of Métis people was the incident southwest of Winnipeg at Riviere aux Ilets de Bois. This little stream originated south of Portage la Prairie and meandered southwards across the prairie through meadows and bluffs (îlets de bois) and drained into the large marsh just west of the Red River and north of the United States — Canada border. It was an area rich in large game, situated in ideal wildfowl country and had good water supplies, as well as abundant fuel and timber for building. As it was on a main route to the buffalo hunting areas, it had been used for years by the Métis for "sugaring"; that is, tapping the tree known as the Manitoba Maple for the purpose of collecting sap to be made into sugar.

Signs of occupation of the land were abundant in the area but, nevertheless, in 1871, a body of Ontario immigrants moved in and settled the land, while all the Métis were away on the annual buffalo hunt. Upon returning, the Métis pointed out that it was their land but the Canadians refused to move. The Métis organized to route the settlers by force and only the intervention of Lieutenant-Governor Archibald presented the start of a small war. Certain that they would not receive justice in the courts of law, the Métis gave way and the Canadians remained as owners of the land, where their descendants

97

still farm some of the richest land in Manitoba. The anti-French, anti-Catholic settlers renamed the stream the Boyne River, to commemorate a battle in which Protestants defeated Catholics at the Boyne River in Ireland. The name remains to this day, but now commemorates the shameful action of the White settlers.

Some Métis received land grants and derived benefit from them. Those who opened up new settlements at St. Malo and St. Pierre or swelled the existing Métis settlements of St. Anne, Ile-des-Chenes and St. Agathe were, on the whole, successful. The first major French-Canadian immigration was to these areas also and their proximity to people devoted to farming no doubt assisted the Métis in becoming successful farmers. Intermarriage between Métis and the French-Canadian immigrants was extensive in these areas and, within two generations, the Métis became absorbed almost wholly into the French culture.

This, then was the social and economic setting from which arose the great trek of the Métis to the Northwest, where they would try to re-establish a lifestyle and once again allow themselves to dream of a New Nation.

The slow migratory movement which oozed out of the Red and Assiniboine River valleys from 1840-1870 became a flood during the decade of 1870-1880. Those who went to the United States tended to congregate in the White Mud River Valley and in settlements in what is now Montana and the Dakotas, where they carried on a lifestyle, the economic base of which, although complemented by farming, trapping and freighting, was the hunting of buffalo. It was this area that offered refuge to Louis Riel during his bitter years of exile from Canada.

Those Métis who moved west out of Manitoba went first to small and already established Métis communities and later developed new settlements such as Petite Ville (1870), St. Laurent (1874), Stobart (1876), Duck Lake (1876), Eugene (1880), Batoche (1881), St. Louis (1882). The South Saskatchewan River was an unsettled area which attracted the largest numbers from Manitoba. Here the old animosities, the fears of White intrusion, the persecutions of 1870 and the land grant problems were kept in the memories of the people more strongly than in any other area in the Northwest.

Having set out in the hope of again leading the old way of life, they were remarkably successful. The herds of buffalo, although diminishing, were still sufficient to satisfy their needs. Families lived in the settlements in the winter and trapped and fished. In the spring, small fields of grain were sown and relatively large garden plots planted with potatoes, turnips, cabbages and onions. Then the men, usually accompanied by their families, went to the plains for the traditional buffalo hunt. Although the importance of agriculture gradually increased, the summer and fall buffalo hunts were kept up and the people could still be classed as partly nomadic.

Missionaries, the Oblate Fathers, worked unceasingly in both the churches and schools which they quickly established in the settlements. The aim of the church was to increase the emphasis on agriculture, but finding it impossible to convince the Métis to abandon the buffalo hunt entirely, the priests encouraged the men to leave their families behind in the villages in order that the children might attend school.

Above all, the missionaries fought the problem of alcohol. It seemed to them that the liquor trade could easily be controlled if they could persuade the Métis to become sedentary farming people and thus come under the constant influence of the church. As more Whites moved onto the plains, alcohol became common as an item of trade. Quarrels, fights, and murders were the usual outcome when a buffalo-hunting group came in contact with a whiskey pedlar. The whiskey that was used in the fur trade was not the bland liquid consumed by modern man. "Indian" or "trade" whiskey could be made in many ways but the most common recipe called for one gallon of raw alcohol mixed with three gallons of water. To this was added a pound of tea, one pound of shredded black chewing tobacco, a quart of black molasses, a handful of red peppers and a scoop of ginger. Little wonder that the Indians called it "fire water". Drinking this vile concoction caused White and Indians and Métis to rapidly lose all control of self and, with minds seemingly deranged, to commit foolish and despicable acts. One man said:

> I never knowed what made an Injun so crazy when he drunk till I tried his booze . . . With a few drinks of this trade whiskey the Missouri looked like a creek and we spur off in it with no fear. It sure was a brave maker, and if a hand had enough of this booze you couldn't drown him. You could even shoot a man through the brain or heart and he wouldn't die until he sobered up.

In the St. Laurent area of Saskatchewan, the Métis formed their own elected government, with Gabriel Dumont as President and eight elected councillors. The rigid rules of the buffalo hunting brigades formed the basis for law and order as well as for the administration of justice. Captains and soldiers enforced the laws of the council and carried out the sentences given lawbreakers. The laws governed the size and shape of farms, regulated ferry service on the river, set out guidelines to govern workers and employers, enforced the observance of the Sabbath, provided for the organization and construction of schools and controlled the planning and organization of the collective buffalo hunts.

Some of the Métis reverted completely to the nomadic lifestyle of the Plains Indians. These Red River people joined with Métis groups who had lived such a life for generations. They had been free and prosperous and would remain so, as long as there were buffalo and the hides commanded a high price. Migrations of these Métis, now increased in number by the exodus from Red River, were governed by the movements of the buffalo herds and both men and animals wandered back and forth across the boundary line between Canada and the United States. Missionaries recorded one hundred and fifty families at Wood Mountain one winter. The banks of the White Mud River were another favored spot for the wandering Métis. The Cypress Hills, Touchwood Hills, the valley of the Red Deer River, the *coulées* around Moose Jaw, the turtle Mountains and the Milk River basin were well populated with buffalo and thus with the nomadic Métis also. As the Métis mixed with the French in Manitoba and became culturally French, in like manner the nomadic Métis of the plains mixed with the Indians and became culturally like them. Indians accepted them as brothers and the Government of Canada registered many of them as Indians when treaties were signed.

As the Métis flowed to and fro across the border, they moved from Canada, where the North West Mounted Police attempted to control the liquor traffic, to the wide open lawlessness of the western United States. The sale of liquor to Indians and Métis, although illegal, was in fact, unrestricted south of the border and there can be little doubt that both groups were almost completely demoralized by alcohol. Theft, rape and murder were common incidents. Everything was sold, including wives and daughters as prostitutes, to secure alcohol. The main source of money, and the reason the liquor traders were in the country, were the buffalo hides. The moral regression which the trade in hides for alcohol brought about concealed a second and more dangerous trap. It tied the Métis to a way of life which would disappear as rapidly as the buffalo did. Rather than effecting a transition to an agricultural settled life, as did the Métis of the settlements, they regressed to a lifestyle which, when it could not longer exist, exposed them to a state of misery and apathy that in a hundred years would still characterize many of them.

The exodus of the Métis from the province of Manitoba in the years 1870·— 1880 was both a blessing and a curse. The Métis people experienced both successes and failures in Manitoba and the Northwest during this period. In Manitoba, the Métis who remained played an important role in the rapidly developing province.

James McKay, the Métis son of a servant of the Hudson's Bay Company, became one of Manitoba's wealthiest and most influential men. He had first worked for the Bay and later became an independent trader. Early in life, he built the famous Deer Lodge Mansion as his home along the banks of the Assiniboine. He owned thousands of acres of land, and , at one time, had a stable of horses valued at $100,-000. This huge, 340-pound man was a most impressive person in every way. His strength was legendary and the stories about him legion. Once, when riding on the plains, he was attacked by a prairie grizzly bear, a species that preyed on the buffalo herds and is now extinct. McKay responded to the attack by lassoing the bear and subduing it. On another occasion, he came upon a man and woman in a horse-drawn cart that had become stuck in the mud. McKay unhitched the horse, put himself between the shafts, and pulled the vehicle out. As a member of the Palliser expedition, which was making a preliminary study of agricultural potential and other related matters on the prairies, McKay is said to have ridden a buffalo. In a spirit of adventure, he rode alongside a huge bull, leaped onto its back, stayed on through vicious bucking, and then regained the saddle of his horse, which had faithfully kept close to the buffalo. People naturally expected a huge man to be slow moving, so McKay took great delight in astonishing friends by leaping over the back of his horse. He was also considered a champion dancer of the Red River Jig, a dance that demanded grace and agility to perform well. It is recorded that he often wore out a pair of moccasins in one night of dancing. A number of Cree and Saulteaux Indians chose McKay, admired by all people, as a family name when they converted to Christianity.

McKay's reaction to the uprising led by Louis Riel in 1869-70 reveals the typical English-speaking half-breed view of the insurrection. Although some English half-breeds supported Riel, the majority tried to remain neutral because of their close ties with both the French-speaking half-breeds and the British crown. Many did not actively support the Canadians. McKay said, "I am loyal to my Queen, but I will not take up arms against Louis Riel's men, many of whom are related to me and my wife."

When Treaty One was being negotiated with the Indians, he was chosen the interpreter because of his complete mastery of English, French, Cree and Saulteaux. At one time in the negotiations, it appeared that the Indians would not only refuse to sign but that an outbreak of violence might occur. Late at night, a speedy messenger was sent from Lower Fort Garry to Deer Lodge. McKay responded by driving all night to reach the Fort and then, in a marathon, four-hour speech, managed to persuade the Indians to continue to negotiate. The Indians later blamed McKay for deceiving them, but such a charge is not supported by the facts. James McKay wrote Ottawa on several occasions in the years following the signing of the treaties and condemned the government for not living up to the promises he, as interpreter, had passed on to the Indians. He was also the major interpreter for Treaties Two and Three.

James McKay rose in politics and became the Honourable James McKay when he was made a member of the Executive Council of the new province.

James McKay should be given a special place in the pages of history for his role in preserving the buffalo. Realizing that buffalo were becoming scarce, McKay had some calves captured and he raised a thriving herd of buffalo at Deer Lodge. The offspring of this private herd, later split and sold to Donald A. Smith, a private citizen, and Colonel Bedson of Stony Mountain Penitentiary, were used to stock Assiniboine Park in Winnipeg and Banff National Park. From McKay's original herd have come many of the buffalo in parks throughout North America.

Another successful Métis family that remained in Manitoba was that of John Norquay, the first native premier of the province. His role in the protection of the linguistic, religious and educational rights of the French-speaking Métis was equalled only by the firm stand he took towards having the various recial groups represented in the government. Without John Norquay, a man of mixed-blood who had experienced racism and social humiliation because of his ancestry, the government's attitude towards the many ethnic groups entering the province would not have been as fair and just as it was. An imposing building which houses government offices in down town Winnipeg is named the "Norquay Building", in honor of his contribution.

Another Métis who deserves a place of honor, not only in the history of West but in that of Canada, is William Kennedy. Strangely enough, this man, born at Cumberland House in 1814 of a Hudson's Bay post manager and a Cree woman named Aggathas, earned his reputation on the ocean, rather than on the prairies. William Kennedy, at age eleven, was sent to Scotland to obtain an education. At eighteen, he returned to Canada to become a clerk in the Hudson's Bay Company, but left their employ in 1846 because he disagreed with the policy of using liquor in the fur trade.

At this time, the world was intrigued by the disappearance of Sir John Franklin in the Canadian Arctic in the year 1846. Twelve expeditions had failed to locate any sign of the explorer or his crew. In 1850, Lady Franklin hired William Kennedy to take charge of another search party. With a crew of seventeen, Kennedy, although not successful in locating Franklin, opened up and mapped new areas of the Arctic and located the northernmost tip of the North American continent. Kennedy's search party showed the world that it was possible to live successfully in the Arctic by adopting the habits and customs of the Eskimos and Indians. He showed that if man worked with nature, rather than against it, survival was possible in the Arctic. Ten more expeditions, a total of twenty-three, were to search for the lost explorer, before a stone cairn was discovered that told of the fate of Franklin and his men.

Returning to Canada, William Kennedy fought to break the monoply of the Hudson's Bay Company on the fur trade in Rupert's Land. His visits to the Red River always attracted large crowds of Whites and mixed-bloods, who trusted him to represent their best interests. Much of the information which Kennedy gathered in the West, he sent to his Métis nephew. Alexander Kennedy Isbister, who carried on the battle of the Métis in London, England. In the 1860's Kennedy came to Red River to retire and built one of the most beautiful stone houses still in existance in Manitoba. It is now a museum. Still active, he was the prime force in starting the *Manitoba Historical and Scien-*

tific Society and was invited to give the first address, the topic of which was *The Northwest Passage*. Three Arctic places have been named in honor of this Métis explorer: Port Kennedy, Kennedy Channel and Cape Kennedy. Twenty years after his death in 1890, a brass plaque in honor of Captain William Kennedy was placed on the wall of St. Andrew's Church, north of Winnipeg. Sir Ernest Shackelton, the famous Antarctic explorer, came to Winnipeg for the dedication. In the National Portrait Gallery in London, England, Kennedy's portrait hangs among the great of British history.

There is really no end to the number of prominent Métis who were in the group that did not take part in the exodus westwards. Of those who did move West, or had always been part of the old Métis lifestyle, a large number achieved greatness but are less well known because of the lack of documentation of their deeds.

Representative of Métis who continued to live the old lifestyle in the Northwest was Jerry Potts, a man who should be acclaimed as a national hero of Canada. Jerry Potts, born about 1840, was the son of a clerk of the American Fur Trade Company, which operated throughout the western United States. His mother was Namo-pisi, a member of the Blood Indians. When his parents were killed, in Jerry's first year, the orphan was raised by two opposite types of persons. For the first five years, Jerry was with Alexander Harvey, one of the most vicious badmen of the Upper Missouri. When his murders became too repulsive even for the frontier, he abandoned Jerry and fled the country, one jump ahead of vigilante groups. The abandoned boy was adopted by Andrew Dawson, a gentle trader of the area. From him Jerry learned English, several Indian languages, the fur trade and allied frontier skills, as well as becoming literate. As a young man in his teens, Potts rejoined his mother's people and drifted around the western United States and Rupert's Land, where his reputation as a great drinker of whiskey was equalled by a rapidly growing reputation as an Indian-style warrior. The Blackfoot honored him as one of the greatest warriors of their tribes. On one occasion, captured by seven members of the Crow Indians, he was taken to their camp. Knowing the Crow language, but not letting his captors become aware of it, Jerry overheard them planning to shoot him in the back. At the warning click of the rifle, Potts threw himself from his saddle, grabbed a gun and shot four of his captors before they could either attack him or flee. Jerry kindly let the remaining three escape his deadly aim.

On occasion, he fought numbers of Sioux warriors and always escaped by doing the unexpected. When chased by two hundred Sioux, the intrepid Potts and his two companions stopped, turned their horses and charged the Sioux. So surprised were the Indians that they forgot to shoot and Potts and his companions rode through their lines unharmed.

George Starr, another Métis, was a great friend of Jerry's. After a bout of heavy drinking, Jerry and George would put on a special performance for spectators. They trimmed each other's moustaches — by shooting their revolvers at each other from a distance of seventy-five feet. The Indians believed that the Métis had supernatural powers but Potts credited it to good shooting resulting from long hours of pratice.

Potts had a number of wives, often at the same time, and always maintained that a man needed several women, but that if fighting was to be avoided a man should marry sisters. Certainly his most successful marriage was that involving the two daughters of a Piegan chief.

From 1868 to 1874, Potts worked for the whiskey traders who were supplying the Indians. It was during this period that he participated in one of the famous battles that occurred between the Blackfoot and the allied Cree and Assiniboines. On October 24, 1870, a group of eight hundred Cree and Assiniboine crept up on a Blood Camp at the Belly River in Alberta and attacked it late in the evening. The Bloods, although losing a few men in the initial burst of firing, put up a good defense. Sending for help during the darkness to a nearby camp of Piegan, of whose presence the Cree and Assiniboines were unaware, the Bloods dug themselves in and waited out the night. When the battle began again in the morning, the hard-pressed Bloods were reinforced by the Piegans, who had with them Jerry Potts and George Starr.

The Cree and Assiniboines retreated to escape the blistering fire of the repeating rifles which the reinforcements possessed. Retreating across the prairie, the Cree and Assiniboines made a last stand in a *coulée* on the edge of the Oldman River, near the present city of Lethbridge. Potts, who was placed in charge, placed some sharpshooters on a nearby hill in such a way that the enemy could not withstand the barrage. At the right psychological moment, Potts led a cavalry charge and the demoralized Crees and Assiniboines fled. When they attempted to cross the Oldman River, the battle came to resemble the butchery of a buffalo hunt. Potts later remarked in an interview, twenty years later, with the *Lethbridge News*, that "you could shoot with your eyes shut and kill a Cree."

Of those who successfully crossed the river, safety still eluded them, for the Blackfoot followed and continued shooting. The final count was forty Piegans and Bloods dead and over three hundred Cree and Assiniboine killed, with countless wounded.

It was battles like this, coupled with the demoralizing traffic in liquor, that brought about the government's determination to establish law and order in the West and the subsequent formation of the North West Mounted Police. Perhaps Jerry Potts had become sickened by the senseless slaughter for, in 1874, at age thirty-seven, he eagerly accepted a job as scout and interpreter for the North West Mounted Police. As their chief scout, he led them to their first great exploits in the West. His first task was to guide them on an attack of the whiskey traders at Fort Whoop-Up.

> He won the confidence of all ranks the first day out and when morning came he rode boldly in front of the advance guard. It was noon when the party reached Milk River and found him there sitting near a fat buffalo cow which he had killed and dressed for the use of the force. To those new to such life he appeared to know everything.[3]

It was Potts who was assigned to travel from tribe to tribe, explaining why the Mounted Police were in the country, and it was he who brought all the major chiefs to meet Colonel McLeod. It was Potts who instructed McLeod in Indian etiquette, so that pipe smoking, praying, sitting around a camp fire and shaking hands was done correctly and with a dignity that indicated to the Indians that the Mounted Police were men who respected the Indian and his culture. It was Potts who led police detachments to safety when they were caught out on the prairies during howling blizzards. It was Potts who interpreted for the Canadian Government when Treaty Eight was negotiated. It was also Potts, a man of few words, who was Colonel McLeod's interpreter. Once, a group of starving Indians came to McLeod and the chief spoke at length and with fervent eloquence. The practical Jerry interpreted the long speech by turning to McLeod and saying: "He wants grub." When several prominent chiefs came to McLeod bearing gifts, which they presented only after lengthy oratory, Potts summed up the entire proceedings for McLeod by the brief interpretation: "Dey damn glad you're here." Jerry did not indulge in idle conversation. Once, when leading a detachment of Mounties through the rolling foothills of Alberta, the weary greenhorns from the East wondered if the hills would ever end. The sergeant in charge rode up to Potts, who was guiding them, and asked hopefully, "What do you think is over the next hill?" Jerry glanced at him rather disdainfully and said: "Another hill". He then spurred his horse away from the sergeant and such frivolous conversation.

It was also Potts, still a heavy drinker, who guided the police to a whiskey trader, helped to arrest him and then rode in the cart containing the impounded whiskey on the long trip back to Fort McLeod. Upon arrival, the embarrassed Mounties had to release the prisoners, for they discovered the cart held an unconscious Jerry, who had drunk all the evidence. His virtues outnumbered his sins, however, and Colonel Steele wrote:

> He was the man who had trained the best scouts in the force and, in the earlier days when the prairie was a trackless waste, there were few trips or expeditions of importance that were not guided by him or the men he had taught in the craft of the plains. As scout and guide I have never met his equal; he had none in either the Northwest or the States to the south . . . Pott's influence with the Blackfoot tribes was such that his presence on many occasions prevented bloodshed.[4]

At Jerry Pott's death in 1896 he was buried with full military honors by the North West Mounted Police. Only in the histories and stories of the Mounted Police has this Métis been suitably honored. Most Canadian people, including the Métis, unfortunately have never heard of him.

McKay, Norquay, Kennedy and Potts are indicative of the important roles played by Métis after the West became a part of Canada.

The New Nation had split into three separate groups in this period of history. Approximately half had elected to remain in the newly created province of Manitoba and to struggle for a place in the new society. Within this group, many were extremely successful and slow assimilation into the English and French-speaking groups began to change their lifestyle. A sub-section of this group moved outside the boundaries of the province to form small settlements along the lakes of Manitoba, where they became fishermen and trappers. The second group reverted to completely nomadic life on the plains and did so in conjunction with the Indians. The process of assimilation was as inevitable for them as for those left behind in Manitoba. The main difference was that they were so rapidly assimilated into the Indian culture that they were soon indistinguishable from them. The third group, those who had fled to the central and northern parts of what is now Saskatchewan and Alberta, retained the semi-settled lifestyle of small farmers and buffalo hunters. They continued to see themselves as a unique people and clung to the ideal of the New Nation. From this group would come the impetus for the Northwest Rebellion of 1885.

GABRIEL DUMONT

BÉRARD

8

The North-West
Rebellion

The beginning of the decade of the 1880's witnessed a growth of nationalism amongst Canadians. Canada's British ties had made Canadians proud to be part of such a vast and powerful empire. Canadians could face any nation with pride and on a basis of equality, as part of the British Empire. Loyalty to the Crown and to the Empire united the country. Discontent with aspects of Confederation on the part of some people was ignored. By the middle of the 1880's, however, Canada found itself in a state of turmoil. English-speaking Canadians questioned Quebec's special status in Confederation and Ontario took upon itself the role of defender of Confederation, as a dominantly English union. The resulting racial and linguistic tensions which developed during this period still plague Canada today.

In the North-West Territories, the 1880's opened with great optimism on the part of the inhabitants. Immigration was the order of the day and, suddenly, western Canada found itself being flooded by an influx of settlers coming to settle the "free" land. They came from the United States and Ontario. Settlements expanded into populous towns. Winnipeg grew to be a city of ten thousand. Of greater importance was the sudden influx of settlers into Saskatchewan, Alberta, and Assiniboia — which were at that time divisions within the North-West Territories. Apart from the area between Battleford and Fort Calgary, which was Indian territory, land was available for settlement.

This sudden immigration to the West resulted largely from the efforts of one man, Lord Lorne. In 1881, he took Canadian and British

111

newspaper men throughout the West and showed them the beautiful, fertile and vast plains that were available for settlement. Though Palliser, during his expedition of 1857-58, had claimed that it was not suitable for agriculture, others after him had contended the opposite. The stage had been set for vast immigration.

During the election campaign of 1878, Sir John A. Macdonald had exploited the growing Canadian nationalism by campaigning on the issue of a National Policy. This policy incorporated the following ideas: (a) protective tariffs (b) the building of the Canadian Pacific Railway to the Pacific Ocean, and (c) settlement of the West.

During the period prior to Confederation, Macdonald had envisioned a nation from "sea to sea". Now that his dreams had been accomplished (British Columbia joined in 1871), it was for the government to decide what steps it would take to fulfill the dream of a nation extending from the Atlantic to the Pacific. Immigration to the West was needed to fill in the empty spaces between and thus consolidate Confederation. An economic factor made agricultural development of the West necessary also, for settlement guaranteed the survival of the Canadian Pacific Railway by creating produce and people to be transported. Western Canada would then become a market for tariff-protected industries in the East and the ensuing surge of business would benefit all concerned. However, by 1884, the Canadian Pacific Railway was in a state of financial crisis and its future was in doubt. The government found it politically feasible to come to the company's rescue largely because of events that occurred in Western Canada. Without the North-West Rebellion, the future of the C.P.R. would have been jeopardized. As a result of the Rebellion, the C.P.R. found a new reason for existence — the transportation of soldiers and supplies to the battlefront.

While Canada was extending its area of influence into the North-West Territories, the Métis regarded this intrusion with fear. The episode of Red River (1869-70) still was fresh in their minds. They remembered that their exodus from Red River was caused basically by mass immigration from Ontario. They also remembered the government fiasco concerning land grants and the persecution by the Canadian militia. Above all, they remembered the fate of their leader, Louis Riel.

In the 1880's, old fears were once again awakened by mass immigration. The arrival of the railroad and steamships and the government's inability to deal with land claims of the Métis disrupted the traditional lifestyle.

To the Federal Government, the immediate needs of the Métis and Indians were not as important as the need to consolidate confederation. After all, the government had established reserves of land for the Indians and had signed treaties with them. The basic problem was that the government had not anticipated the rapid extinction of the buffalo. This, plus the extreme difficulty encountered in trying to make the Indians into farmers, resulted in the near-starvation of people on reserve after reserve. Famine, malnutrition and disease brought many bands to the verge of extinction. Despite reports of increasing restlessness amongst the tribes in the North-West Territories, the government seemed incapable of taking the problems seriously.

The Métis, however had not been given reserves or free supplies of food. Paradoxically, this was, perhaps, a blessing, for they managed to survive and to retain a degree of independence on their small farms after the disappearance of the buffalo in 1884. However, the Métis in Saskatchewan still faced the same problem they had faced at Red River in 1869-70. The people had difficulty in comprehending the European concept of land ownership and the legal implications of individual title. As at Red River, the Métis lived on land that belonged, in law, to the Crown. They were, in fact, squatters. Although they had requested individual land titles, the government persisted in refusing to deal with the matter. As surveying of the North-West Territories proceeded slowly, people from the "East" moved in and homesteaded the land. Unfortunately the land surveyed and allocated to them often cut across traditional Métis land. To add insult to injury, three Métis who had been Riel's foes at Red River, were responsible for the granting of land titles in Saskatchewan. They apparently sympathized little with their fellow Métis in Saskatchewan and followed government policy regarding land sales, even when such actions transgressed upon the rights of the squatters.

In the latter part of 1884, land surveyors appeared around Battleford and the fears and tensions within the Métis communities reached a climax. Petition after petition was fowarded to Ottawa pleading for a resolution of Métis land claims. Ottawa ignored them.

Remembering the victory at Red River, the Métis turned to their only political hero, Louis Riel. It is true that they had Gabriel Dumont, but he could neither read nor write and was as helpless as the rest in trying to deal with legal and political problems. What the Métis needed was not a rifleman, but an educated and charismatic leader. A delegation of four men was chosen to ride to Montana and request Riel to return to Saskatchewan to aid his people.

What the Métis of the Saskatchewan Territory did not realize was that Riel had become a changed person. The Riel of 1884 was not the same as the Riel of 1870. Tremendous pressures had been imposed upon him during his fifteen years' absence from Canada. After the execution of Thomas Scott, and following the Insurrection of 1870, Riel had become the focus of political agitation in both Ontario and Quebec. Though elected three times to the House of Commons between the years 1870-1875, he dared not sit as a member, for fear that his life would be taken, for the province of Ontario had placed a five thousand dollar price on his head. Bounty hunters sought him everywhere. Furthermore, his amnesty had been granted only under the condition that Riel accept a period of exile for five years. Thus, the man who had fought so hard to keep the Northwest in Canadian hands was forced to leave his country and become a fugitive.

Since he could not remain within Canada, Riel initially established himself in St. Paul from where he could keep watch on the events in Manitoba. Unfortunately, the news he received depressed him. Lepine, one of his comrades in the resistance, was in jail awaiting trial for the execution of Scott. Winnipeg had been incorporated as a city, with a majority Anglo-Saxon population. After several attempts on his life, Riel realized he was not safe at St. Paul so he moved under an assumed name to Montreal.

Montreal should have been ideal for Riel. He had studied there as a young man and knew many people. The people with whom he associated, however, were caught up in an intense religious-political debate based upon the concept of Ultramontanism. Ultramontanism meant the rigid segregation of people by religious faith and the alliance of church and state to ensure it. "State" in the Canadian Ultramontane movement meant the province of Quebec, for it represented the French language and culture and the Roman Catholic religion. The leader of the movement was Mgr. Bourget, the Bishop of Montreal. Bishop Bourget met with Riel on several occasions during this period and each made a lasting impression upon the other. Bourget encouraged Riel to believe that his mission in life was to regenerate his people, the Métis.

114

Riel soon found himself caught up with this "holy war" of Catholics versus Catholics and Catholics versus Protestants. Within this period, a dramatic change occurred in Riel. He suddenly began to blame many of his problems on the Roman Catholic religion. Seeing the dissension that occurred within his religion, he began to dream of a new French-Catholic state in the North-West Territories. In his subsequent travels in the United States, where he attempted to gain support from the government and Franco-Americans for assistance to the Métis, Riel became a greater advocate of Ultramontanism. He appealed to Franco-Americans to settle in the Canadian West and to assure the "victory of the French-Canadians" in the land of the Métis.

In December of 1874, while sitting on a hilltop near Washington, Riel had a vision.

> . . . the same spirit who showed himself to Moses in the midst of the burning cloud appeared to me in the same manner. I was stupified. I was confused. He said to me, 'Louis David Riel, you have a mission to fulfill." Stretching out my arms and bowing my head, I received the heavenly message.[1]

Mgr. Bourget knew of and encouraged Riel's dream of establishing a French-Catholic state in the West. Furthermore, Bourget had led Riel to believe that such was his ordained mission. This vision, then, could have occurred or could have been created by Riel in a moment of tension and internal strife. Perhaps Riel could not distinguish between mysticism and reality. As a product of the plains, he may have tended to mix the Indian world of dreams and visions with his knowledge of the Christian religion. Certainly, he believed in signs and prophesied from them.

While attending mass in Washington in the United States of America, Riel became hysterical and had to be removed from the church. His instability grew worse and, in January of 1876, Riel was taken to Keeseville for observation of his mental state. In March, he was brought to Longue Point, Quebec, and placed in the mental asylum there. Riel had changed and so had his name. He was now Louis David. In May of that year, he moved once again, this time to Beauport. There, he was registered as La Rochelle. Either Riel chose those names himself or the hospital authorities did so to protect him from investigators and possible humiliation and imprisonment, for he was still supposedly in exile and subject to arrest if found in Canada. Riel remained at Beauport insane asylum until 1878.

While there, he continued his correspondence with Mgr. Bourget who continued to reinforce Riel's dream of the mission he must accomplish.

Upon his release as a cured man, the Métis leader went to Carroll in the heart of the Métis country in the United States. When Riel arrived, he was shocked at the illicit whiskey trade that was slowly destroying the Métis and Indians. He requested the American government to set aside a reserve for the Métis, where they might be protected from the influence of alcohol. His request was not granted.

While in Montana, Riel met Marguerite Monet dit Bellehumeur whom he married *à la mode du pays*. They were officially married on March 9, 1882 by Father Damiani, a Jesuit priest from St. Peter's, a town that was some one hundred and fifty miles west. A child was born to them in May, 1882. As a married man with responsibilities, Riel had to find some means of support and accepted Father Damiani's request that he come and teach at St. Peter's mission.

While in Montana, Louis Riel continued to fight for a better life for the Métis in the United States. He fought the whiskey traders and pressed charges against them in the courts. The case was lost, for the courts ruled that Métis were not Indians and that the legal restrictions concerning liquor and the Indians did not apply to them. Of particular interest was the principle established by the United States courts that a significant difference did exist between the Indians and Métis.

In the United States elections of 1882, Riel, now an American citizen, threw himself into the campaign with enthusiasm. He allied himself with the Republican party, for it promised to right many of the injustices inflicted upon the Métis. Following a close contest in which a recount of ballots were necessary to decide the winner, Riel was charged with manipulating the Métis voters. In the newspaper battles which followed, Riel wrote a number of letters to leading Montana papers in which he defended his role in the election. Such letters show that Louis Riel used the term "half-breed" when writing in English and "Métis" when using French.[2]

This, then was the new Riel whom the four Métis from Saskatchewan asked to return to Canada to assist the Canadian Métis. He was a man who had been exiled from his homeland, been pursued by bounty hunters, had a nervous breakdown, spent a period of time in an asylum for the insane, been cured, joined his Métis brethren in Montana and had become an American citizen and a political figure of importance in Montana.

When the four Métis, Gabriel Dumont, Moise Oullette, Michel Dumas and James Isbister pleaded with Louis Riel to return, he was eager to accept the invitation. He had a mission to fulfill and his people had called:

> We, the French and English natives of the North-West, know that Louis Riel made a bargain with the Government of Canada, in 1870, which said bargain is contained mostly in what is known as the "Manitoba Act", have thought it adviseable that a delegation be sent to said Louis Riel, and have his assistance to bring all the matters referred to in the above resolutions in a proper shape and form before the Government of Canada, so that our just demands be granted.[3]

Upon his arrival at Batoche, Riel realized that he had lost no prestige among his people. Indeed, he was greeted as a returning hero. He set out immediately to organize the Whites, Indians and Métis. All three groups responded warmly to him.

Riel's first attempt at making Ottawa realize the plight of the people in the North-West Territories was carried out with reserved moderation. At no time did Riel advocate armed conflict. He went about presenting and writing petitions on behalf of the people, all people, in the hope that Ottawa would listen to their grievances. Many members of Riel's supporters were more impatient and wanted quick action. The most impatient was Gabriel Dumont.

Dumont was born at Red River in 1837. His father had been a farmer and a freighter. Around 1840, Gabriel's father moved from Red River to the Fort Pitt-Fort Edmonton region, where he began trading with the Indians. It was within this area that Gabriel Dumont learned the arts or horseback riding, buffalo hunting and marksmanship with a rifle.

At the tender age of eleven, Gabriel proved his manhood. His father, having decided to leave the Fort Pitt-Fort Edmonton region for Red River, took his young son along. One evening after camping for the night, Gabriel heard a distant rumbling. Fearing that it was the Blackfoot galloping in to attack, he awoke the camp. Fortunately for all, Dumont had heard, not the Blackfoot, but the earth-shaking rumble of a stampeding buffalo herd. His show of courage and disciplined behaviour would have saved the camp had it truly been the Blackfoot. His reward, the gift of a gun, was given to him by his uncle, Alexis

Fisher. The gift of a gun was symbolic in the West. By it, one understood that a boy had achieved the status of manhood.

Gabriel Dumont could neither read nor write, but he was a gifted military leader. Having fought Indian wars and hunted buffalo, he was accustomed to action and was impatient with Riel's policy of moderation. It is easy to understand why Dumont was impatient and less easy to understand the initial moderation of Riel. The people, both Indian and Métis, were literally starving to death. The White settlers were better off but were concerned about the question of legal title to their lands. There is reason to believe that during this period a considerable affinity existed between the three groups and that the White settlers sympathized with the sufferings of the Indians and Métis.

The Benton *Weekly Record* reported that Canadian Cree Indians had wandered across the boundary into the United States in search of food.

> They were selling their guns and every other article of value to procure food, while women were prostituting themselves, to save their children from starvation.[4]
>
> *   *   *
>
> The men were weak and emaciated from hunger, and women and children with rags and filth . . . The country is entirely destitute of game . . . the only hope these unfortunate wretches can have to save themselves from speedy death is to shake hands with the Sioux and become enemies of the whites.[5]

The plight of the nomadic Métis was equally pathetic. The semi-settled, farming Métis were better off, but feared they would become equally poverty-stricken unless legal title to their small farms could be secured.

After a round of public meetings, it became apparent that the Métis demands, greatly modified by Riel, were fourfold: free title to land presently held by the people; provincial status for the Districts of Saskatchewan, Assiniboia and Alberta; the setting up of laws to encourage the agricultural settlement of the nomadic Indians and Métis; and more liberal treatment of the Indians. With the mass of the population on his side, Riel completed a petition and sent it to Ottawa on December 16, 1884.

Realizing that the power was now held by Riel and fearful of some of his religious views, the Catholic clergy turned against him. Religious, social and financial pressures were brought to bear on him in an effort to force him to return to the United States. The only result

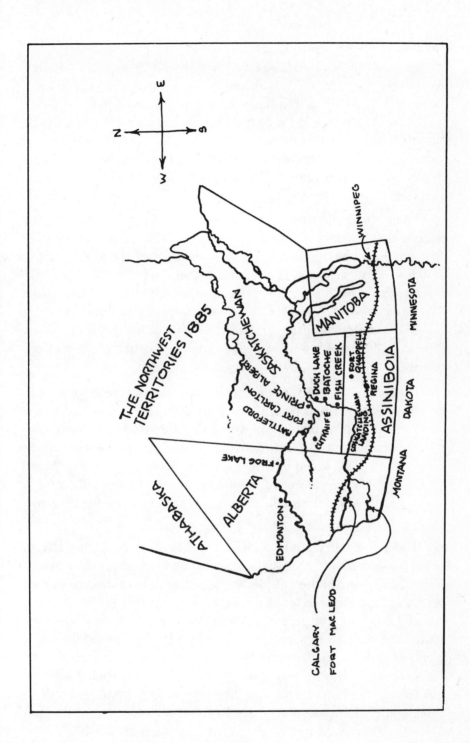

THE NORTHWEST TERRITORIES 1885

ATHABASKA

ALBERTA

SASKATCHEWAN

PRINCE ALBERT

FORT CARLTON

BATTLEFORD

MANITOBA

ASSINIBOIA

MINNESOTA

DAKOTA

MONTANA

WINNIPEG

DUCK LAKE
BATOCHE
FISH CREEK
CUT KNIFE
SASKATOON
LANDING
FORT
QU'APPELLE
REGINA

FROG LAKE

EDMONTON

CALGARY

FORT MAC LEOD

was that Louis Riel became anti-clerical in his attitude. He began to indulge in violent outbursts against the Catholic Church. Describing himself as a prophet who would lead the New Nation to freedom, he denounced the clergy as unchristian and more interested in the institution of the church than in the people that it was designed to serve. Riel informed the clergy that he would establish a new church in Western Canada, with Bishop Bourget of Montreal as Pope. He began to have visions of an Utopia to be established in the North West Territories, where all nationalities and religions would live in peace.

Under the leadership of Father André, the Church hoped to displace Riel as leader of the Métis — to no avail. The clergy then tried to dissuade the Métis from following Riel, but discovered that their faith in him was too strong. Riel informed Father André that the Federal Government owed him a personal sum of $100,000. He claimed that this amount would repay his loss of prestige, his years of exile and, above all, his lost property at Red River. Until his claims and the claims of all the Métis were settled, he had no intention of leaving the country.

On February 4, 1885, a telegram from Ottawa was received which stated that the petition from the people of the Territories had been received and that a commission would be established to "investigate claims of half-breeds." The first step, to be undertaken at an unstated time in the future, would be a census of the Métis in the North-West Territories. The people were disappointed and angered by such an indecisive approach to the problems that they had expressed for so many years.

Having achieved nothing, Riel had begun to doubt his effectiveness as a leader. The thought of returning to Montana entered his mind. To reassure himself of Métis support, he called a meeting of the people around Batoche to decide whether or not they wished him to stay. By this time, the people had become very disenchanted with the attitude of the government and had little hope of a peaceful settlement. Abandoned by their priests and in danger of losing their lands, the settlers at Batoche had only one hope — Louis Riel. They requested that he remain and lead them. At similar meetings in other communities, Riel was reassured of the support of the people. The Métis saw him as their prophet, the divinely inspired "David" of the New Nation.

Confident once more, Riel established a provisional government on March 19, with Pierre Parenteau as President and Gabriel Dumont as Adjutant-General.[6] As in Manitoba in 1869-70, everyone realized Riel was the real leader.

During the winter, tension had also continued to mount amongst the Indians. The Department of the Interior budget had been cut by $140,000. This meant less food and clothing for the already starving Indians. With all aspects of decision-making centralized in Ottawa, the Indian agents found it impossible to react to the constantly recurring crises on the reserves. For the Indians, the lack of decisive action created more hardships and pain, as many requisitions for food were turned down by the Indian agents. If they were approved locally, someone else in the Department in Ottawa would reject the demand. A high death rate soon developed among Indian people, as starvation and disease took their toll.

Although informed of the hardships imposed by the budget restrictions, the government persisted in cutting the expenditures. There is some reason to believe that by attempting to do so, the government hoped to force the Indians to turn more readily to agriculture as a way of life. By 1884, the Indians had also come to realize the implications of the treaties and the reserve system. Not until they were placed on reserves and every aspect of their lives was controlled by a government agent, did they realize that they had lost their independence. Gone was their roaming way of life. Gone were the buffalo. Immigrants were rapidly settling the land and these things the Indians had not anticipated. They had imagined that the land would be used by both Indians and Whites and that all peoples would live side by side and prosper. Such was not the case. Clashes with the North West Mounted Police occurred. Big Bear, an Indian chief who had refused to sign Treaty No. 6, became the leader of the Indians who sought better terms from the Federal Government. By 1885, the Indians had come to realize that their problems were also those of the Métis. Land, immigration, and food shortages were problems common to both. It was natural, then, that the Indians should also turn to Riel as their spokesman.

At Batoche, Riel had resolved to set his provisional government in motion. It had not been established for more than a few days when the Métis leader discovered that he no longer had the active support of the English-speaking half-breeds. They had supported Riel in his petitions and demands but a Provisional Government backed by armed men smacked of treason to them. Neutrality, rather than assistance, was what the English half-breeds offered Riel. Not only was the support of the English half-breeds lost, but the Roman Catholic Church was now hopelessly alienated. The priests were thrust out of their churches and denied a role in the New Nation. Henceforth Riel's own religious views would predominate. The fateful decision had been made. The majority of the English half-breeds had declared their neutrality. The White settlers wanted nothing of armed rebellion and now opposed Riel. The French-speaking half-breeds from Manitoba, Assiniboia and Alberta were not flocking to assist their brethren at Batoche and the moderating influence of the priests had been rejected. Armed conflict by a minority appeared inevitable.

The fighting began at Duck Lake. On March 26, Major Crozier, with fifty-six Mounted Police and forty-one volunteers, marched out of Fort Carlton to arrest Riel. The Métis, under the leadership of Gabriel Dumont, met them at Duck Lake. The site into which Dumont lured the Mounted Police favored the Métis style of fighting. With the Police in a shallow valley, the Métis used the cover of the ravines and the woods to conceal their presence. Dumont allowed Crozier to march into what was pratically the centre of the valley. Alerted by his scouts to possible danger, Crozier ordered a halt, neatly in the centre of the trap laid by Dumont. Two horsemen, Isidore Dumont and Falling Sand, a Cree Indian, came riding toward the police detachment. Believing that these two horsemen wished to parley, Crozier set out to meet them. While all this was going on, the Métis with some Indians, unobtrusively surrounded the police. Suddenly aware of the probability of an ambush, the police force set up a barricade with their sleighs. Crozier, accompanied by a scout named McKay, met the two representatives of the Métis and extended his hand in friendship to the unarmed Indian. Mistaking the gesture as a sign of aggression, Falling Sand made a grab for McKay's rifle. McKay fired and Isidore Dumont fell dead from his saddle. The battle at Duck Lake had begun.

Muzzle loaders fired volley upon volley. The police force, surrounded on three sides, were easy prey for the Métis sharpshooters. After forty minutes of battle, ten policemen lay dead and eleven had been wounded. Crozier saw the futility of continued fighting and saw the need to withdraw his men to a safer position. Ordering his men to retreat, Crozier hoped to return in relative safety to Fort Carleton with the remainder of his force. It is thanks to Riel that the police and volunteers were not annihilated. Dumont was ready to follow Crozier and his troops with the aim of killing or capturing all of them. Riel refused Dumont's request to do so as he felt that too much blood had been shed already.

Word of Crozier's loss reached other settlements. That the Mounties had been defeated was greeted with joy in the Métis settlements, but had its greatest influence upon the Indians. It proved to them that the Whites were not invincible in battle. The call to war and vengeance was soon heard amongst the Indian tribes throughout the North West Territories. Only in Saskatchewan was it heeded.

At Battleford, a band of two hundred Crees led by Little Pine and Strike-Him-On-The-Back joined an Assiniboine party and ransacked parts of the White settlement. Roughly five hundred settlers, the majority of them women and children, sought the protection of the North West Mounted Police barracks. They watched as warriors looted their homes and burned stores and buildings. For a whole month they were besieged.

At Fort Pitt, the Indians, under the leadership of Big Bear, surrounded the fort in which thirty civilians and twenty Mounted Police had taken up defensive positions. The Indians demanded that clothing and food be issued them and, upon being refused, set up camp nearby and prepared to besiege the fort. However, during the night the civilians and Police were able to make a quiet retreat by boat.

At Frog Lake, Wandering Spirit and a handful of braves killed Thomas Quinn, the Indian Agent, along with the farm instructor. Two priests, Fathers Fafard and Marchand were also killed. The Indians looted and then burned the main buildings.

The incident at Frog Lake became the catalyst which caused the Canadian Government to intervene. Up to this point, Sir John A. Macdonald, either dreadfully ill-informed or simply ignorant of the conditions in the West, had looked upon the events as a mere cry from "ten thousand outcasts." Where petitions had failed to gain Macdonald's attention, the Frog Lake massacre attracted the interest of the government and the public in the rebellion.

Immediately, the government undertook to increase the expenditures of the Department of the Interior on food supplies for the Indians. The generous gifts of food kept the majority of tribes neutral and proved the wisdom of the decision.

The Canadian government took prompt military action, as well. Within a matter of weeks an army of eight thousand had been mobilized and sent to the North-West, under the command of General Middleton. Rapidly transported to the West by railway, the army sent columns to the three key areas of trouble. Colonel Otter marched to the relief of Battleford; Major-General Strange moved against Chief Big Bear and the Crees, while General Middleton committed his efforts to the defeat of the Métis at Batoche.

Gabriel Dumont, with three hundred fifty Métis and a handful of Indians, had the impossible task of defending Batoche. Unlike the government soldiers, who were armed with Snider-Enfield rifles, the Métis still used the old, slow-loading muzzle-loaders and only three-quarters of them had any guns at all. Middleton had cannon, a Gatling gun,[7] and ample supplies of ammunition. It was obvious to Dumont that against such odds there was only one sensible method of warfare — a guerilla type of hit-and-run attack. Riel intervened and ordered Dumont not to harry the approaching troops. His reasoning was that guerilla warfare was the Indian method of fighting, not that of the Métis. There seems little doubt, however, that Riel, a devoutly religious man abhorred killing and used every possible excuse to delay violent action. He still hoped that peaceful negotiations might take place. Riel's stubborn attitude towards bloodshed was beginning to have disastrous results. Middleton's army was allowed to advance towards Batoche in perfect safety. Dumont began to question Riel's ability to handle the problem for he was well aware that prayers would not stop the advancing army.

Meanwhile, the army headed by Major-General Middleton was marching towards Batoche. Dumont, knowing the country well, decided to ambush the soldiers at Fish Creek. Riel was opposed to the plan but this time Dumont insisted upon action. The Métis left Batoche with two hundred men to engage Middleton. Reluctantly Riel accompanied them. Upon reaching the site at which they would make their stand, Riel changed his mind. After a long session of prayer, he challenged Dumont's plans and ordered that the men return to Batoche. Fortunately, at that moment a messenger arrived bearing the rumor, later found to be false, that a detachment of Mounted Police was approaching Batoche from Qu'Appelle. Dumont sent fifty men under Riel's leadership back to Batoche to defend the settlement.

The morning of April 24, was a drab rainy morning. At Fish Creek, twenty-two miles from Batoche, the Métis had dug rifle pits from which they could fire upon Middleton's men. The natural vegetation offered a camouflage that proved to be a major factor in the coming battle. The morning mists allowed a party of Métis unexpectedly to encounter the Canadian soldiers. The element of surprise had been lost and the battle was to be a day-long affair of sporadic raids and long distance firing. The Métis were in control of the one hillside and the ravine itself. Each time the Canadians attacked, their bodies would be silhoutted against the horizon and they were easy targets for the Métis sharpshooters. Middleton's strength was his cannon which, although they did little harm, were weapons frightening to the Métis and Indians. So demoralized by the cannon were the Indians that most of them deserted during the day.

By good shooting and quick raids upon the Canadians, while protected by the smoke of brush and grass fires set by Dumont, the Métis managed to hold their own, even though they were outnumbered eight to one. As the day ended, the Métis counted four dead and two wounded while the soldiers had ten dead and forty wounded. Although the Métis had not won the battle, they had stopped the Canadian advance and considered this to be a moral victory.

Meanwhile, at Batoche, Riel was undergoing serious doubts concerning the decisions he had made. He had come to realize that his mission was in jeopardy. News continued to reach him of masses of troops advancing closer to Batoche. He had messengers sent out to Poundmaker and Big Bear seeking reinforcements, but the Indians were also encountering problems. They had guns but insufficient ammunition, and the Métis could not help, since they also suffered a shortage. When informed that Riel was awaiting them, the Indians set out for Batoche. On their way, they encountered a supply train on its way to Battleford. Taking some twenty-two prisoners and the supplies, Poundmaker's men countinued toward Batoche. Following another brief skirmish with the military scouts, the Indians received news of the siege at Batoche. They made camp in order to discuss a course of action but, before the prolonged council ended, Batoche had been captured.

General Middleton, cautious after the Fish Creek battle, had remained camped for a fortnight in order to give his men time to rest and to allow the wounded to recover. On May 7, he set out for Batoche. Accompanied by the steamer, *Northcote*, on which he placed cannon and thirty-five soldiers in order to attack from the Saskatchewan River, Middleton prepared his strategy. He planned to have the ground troops and the men on the boat attack the town simultaneously.

On May 9, the steamer made its appearance on the river beside Batoche. Dumont, realizing the danger from the armed boat, had the ferry cable lowered as the vessel steamed underneath it, so that the boat's smoke-stack and pilot house were shorn off. Musket fire from the Métis crippled its lower deck and the boat, out of control, drifted for several miles and finally became stuck on a sand bar, where it remained for the duration of the battle at Batoche.

Arriving at the scene of battle with ground troops, Middleton soon became aware that Batoche would be harder to take than he had anticipated. The Métis had prepared well in defence of their heartland. On their left flowed the South Saskatchewan with its steep banks. The approach to the village was surrounded by a line of rifle pits and trenches that extended to the river. The main area of defence was on the slopes of the wooded hills that were parallel to the river.

Realizing the Métis position was almost impregnable, Middleton resorted to "delayed action" fighting. By keeping the Métis occupied over a period of days through frequent skirmishes, he anticipated that the Métis resistance would crumble as their food and ammunition became scarce. He was unaware that his foes were already desperately short of ammunition. By the end of the third day, the Métis supply of ammunition was so low that some had to resort to loading their muzzle loaders and shotguns with nails and pebbles.

On the fourth day, May 12, the Métis met defeat. Colonel Middleton's troops mounted a mass attack upon the rifle pits and trenches, from which the Métis poured out to engage them in hand-to-hand conflict. As the tide of battle turned, those Métis who were able to do so fled to the woods. The Canadian soldiers were surprised at the few defenders that Batoche had had, but were more shocked to discover that the valiant defenders who died fighting included men as old as Jose Oullette, ninety-three, and many youngsters of fourteen and fifteen years of age.

The two leaders of the Métis reacted differently to the changed circumstances. Both were fugitives in the wooded ravines surrounding Batoche. Riel ensured the safety of his wife and children by placing them in a friend's home and then he retreated to the woods for prayers and deliberation concerning future action. There was no thought of trying to escape. In reply to a message from Middleton demanding surrender, Riel stated that he desired his councillors and people to be left free. He would surrender to "fulfill God's will". He would give himself up in order to continue to plead the cause of the Métis before the people and government of Canada. The surrender was accomplished and Riel was incarcerated in the North West Mounted Police barracks in Regina.

Dumont, the man of action, tried without success to rally the Métis and to attempt to recapture Batoche. The sight of looting, burning homes and devastated farmsteads, however, had destroyed the spirit of resistance. Dumont then turned to gathering blankets, food and clothing to distribute to the fugitive women and children who had escaped to caves in the river-bank and gullies in the woods. Hearing that Riel had surrendered, Gabriel Dumont and Michel Dumas determined to flee to the United States. A message from Middleton to surrender was answered in characteristic manner: "Tell Middleton I still have ninety cartridges to use on his men." Almost one year from the date they had gone through Fort Benton to request Riel to return to Canada, the two men were in foreign territory once again, this time as refugees.

However, the rebellion was not yet over. There were still Poundmaker and Big Bear to be dealt with. Upon hearing of Riel's surrender, Poundmaker addressed a letter to Middleton requesting peace terms. In return, Middleton demanded an unconditional surrender and also stated that, since he had made no terms with Riel, he would not do so with Poundmaker. On May 26, Poundmaker and his men surrendered unconditionally to the general.

Big Bear was still at large. During the month of May, he had been busy trying, without success, to restore the unity that had once existed between the Plains and Wood Cree. On May 26, Big Bear received news that a column of troops was near. It was Major-General Strange, whose column had joined with Middleton's army in an effort to capture Big Bear. At the Battle of Red Deer Creek, Strange realized the impossibility of trying to trail and bring to battle Indians who could disappear so rapidly in the woods. He thus retreated, allowing the Indians to make their way in peace into the woodlands. On July 2, Big Bear, out of food and ammunition, surrendered and the rebellion ended.

On July 6, 1885, a charge of treason was laid against Louis Riel. The government hired four of Canada's best lawyers to prepare the case against him. Sympathetic Canadians, who were mainly French from Quebec, formed a Riel Defence Committee and hired lawyers for his defence.

The trial began on July 20. To the charge of treason Riel pleaded not guilty, on the advice of his lawyers. The strategy of his lawyers was to claim Riel was insane and therefore could not be held responsible for his actions. Riel objected strenuously to this. The lawyers secured the permission of the judge not to allow Riel to speak during the progress of the trial. Riel protested in vain.

> I cannot abandon my dignity. Here I have to defend myself against the accusation of high treason, or I have to consent to the animal life of an asylum.[8]

At no time were the lawyers or witnesses allowed to discuss the grievances that led to the rebellion, for the judge ruled that Riel, not the government, was on trial. The testimony of the witnesses, especially that of the priests, was damning. They maintained strongly that Riel was not accountable for his actions and, indeed, had been mentally unbalanced before and during the rebellion. Even the expert witnesses, Dr. Francois Roy of Beauport and Daniel Clark of the Toronto Lunatic Asylum, testified that the prisoner was insane.

As the trial neared its end, Riel was granted permission to speak once to the court. Typically, he began with a moment of prayer. He then reviewed the history of the troubles in the Northwest, beginning with the sufferings of his people, the inaction of the government and the subsequent problems. With dignity, he maintained that he was sane and wanted no acquittal because of a plea of insanity. He did not deny that he had been in an asylum at one time, but emphasized that competent medical men had pronounced him cured. Did visions, prophecies and a sense of mission prove he was insane?

> I believed for years I had a mission . . . I believe I have a mission at this very time.[9]

After the summing-up, the jurors retired. In one hour they returned with a verdict of guilty, but with a recommendation for mercy.

Before passing sentence the judge asked if the prisoner wished to say anything. Riel rose and began to speak by almost thanking the jury for finding him guilty, since such a sentence meant that they had judged him to be sane and thus responsible for his actions.

> Up to this moment I have been considered by a certain party as insane, by another as criminal . . . Today by the verdict of the court one of these situations has disappeared. I cannot fulfill my mission as long as I am looked upon as an insane being . . . the verdict against me is proof that I am a prophet.[10]

Riel ended the speech by saying:

> If I have been astray, I have been astray, but not as an imposter, but according to my conscience.[11]

The judge ruled that Riel must be hanged by the neck until dead on September 18, 1885.

The verdict embroiled all Canada and many parts of the world in heated controversy.

English Canada wondered why a traitor and rebel should have been recommended for mercy. French Canada saw him as the victim of the racial and religious bigotry of an English, Protestant jury. The fact that the English-speaking Jackson, Riel's secretary, was acquitted on the basis of insanity reinforced their view. English Canada demanded his death. French Canada demanded a pardon. Appeals to higher courts and finally to the Supreme Court of Canada were made. All upheld the original decision. The Prime Minister and Cabinet could, however, commute the death penalty. The commutation would be made, not on the basis of legal justice, but according to what was politically expedient. Macdonald, not wanting to antagonize any voters, appointed a commission composed of three doctors to rule on whether Riel was sane or insane. If judged insane, even English Canada would accept having the death sentence commuted. Their unanimous decision was that he was sane but became "unbalanced" when certain political or religious questions were raised.

From around the world came appeals to the Canadian Government to commute the death sentence. The International Arbitration Society cabled an appeal from London, England. From France and the United States came petitions bearing names by the tens of thousands. Quebec talked of secession. Ontario spoke of armed subjection of the French. Tentative suggestions from England of a royal reprieve by Queen Victoria infuriated Macdonald.

> 'He shall hang', said Macdonald, 'though every dog in Quebec bark in his favor'.[12]

The trials of the other alleged rebels had also been completed. Seventy-two had been arrested. Approximately one half were brought to trial and a number were acquitted. Eighteen Métis were convicted of treason and imprisoned. Chiefs Poundmaker and Big Bear each received a three-year sentence. Eight Indians were hanged and three given life imprisonment. However, many of the Cree and Métis had escaped the law by fleeing to Montana, where their descendants live to this day.

The Métis, although defeated, homeless and with many still in hiding, had not forgotten Riel. Gabriel Dumont and Michel Dumas had successfully avoided the Canadian army, crossed the border into the United States, and surrendered to the American troops at Fort Assiniboine. Cleveland, the President of the United States, personally declared them political refugees and ordered them released.

Dumont immediately visited all the Métis communities in the United States and collected money and offers of assistance to arrange the escape of Louis Riel. He established secret relay stations, horses and provisions every ten to twenty miles from Regina, Saskatchewan to Lewiston, Montana, a distance of over four hundred miles. All Métis settlements and Indian villages were alerted. Somehow, news of the plans were received by the North West Mounted Police and the conspiracy failed when the guards at Regina Police Barracks were increased in number.

On November 16, Louis "David" Riel walked with calmness and dignity to the gallows. But even in his last few minutes on earth the prophet of the Métis was to endure persecution. The hangman was Jack Henderson, who had been a prisoner of the Provisional Government in Manitoba in 1870 and who, in 1885, was again a prisoner for three days. He had threatened to kill Riel and as he slipped the hangman's noose over the hooded head of the prisoner he said:

> Do you know me? You cannot escape me today.[13]

The body was placed under the floor of St. Mary's Church at Regina and guarded until December 9. Late at night the coffin was carried to a railroad siding and furtively placed in a box car for secret transportation to St. Vital in Manitoba.

9

Second Métis
Dispersion

The rebellion of 1885 was the last stand of the Old West and the Métis were the primary factor in that West. They were the free hunters standing in opposition to the builders of towns, farmhouses, fences and the destruction of wildlife. Having stood, fought and lost, they dispersed once again; this time, however, there were fewer places to retreat. Wherever they might go, the hordes of incoming settlers would overhwelm them. The desperate, disarrayed retreat was to be a final dispersal; never would the Métis stand and fight again. The Indians accepted the inevitable, allowed themselves to be herded back to their reserves and stayed there. Many of the Métis sought what pockets of emptiness remained: the still unsettled areas of the Western United States, the Peace River country and the wilds in the far north. They travelled on foot, in carts and on horseback as well as by the historic waterways. But wherever they went, the burgeoning forces of the new life would find them. Their day was past. The future belonged to the White settlers with ploughs, not to the Métis with guns and traps.

Fresh in their minds were the horrors of the dead and wounded at Batoche. Rankling in their hearts were the memories of the Canadian soldiers looting and then burning the cabins at Batoche. Still vivid were the cries of hungry children, cries which pierced deeply as the Métis were forced into handing over their guns to the troops and, in so doing, lost their only chance of getting food. Disillusionment with the Church was great, for it, represented by Father Végreville, had acted as agent for the conquerors in collecting the guns. The Métis were only too well aware of their sixty brothers, including the beloved Louis

Riel, who were in prison awaiting trial. Harking back to the persecutions in Manitoba in 1870, many expected new reprisals. Those who left the Saskatchewan River area were driven by fear. Those who stayed were governed by apathy or buoyed by the hope that, because they had not participated in the rebellion, they would not suffer any consequences.

How many moved to the various places it is impossible to tell. Fear caused large numbers to change their names, which makes the task of tracing them almost impossible. Many fled to the United States and joined Métis groups in Montana and the Dakota territories. They knew those areas where the buffalo had been hunted and doubtlessly felt quite at home. President Cleveland of the United States accepted them as political refugees and offered them sanctuary. Meetings were held by the refugees with a view to organizing an attack on the North-West Territories; fortunately, this mad scheme was soon abandoned. Lieutenant-Governor Dewdney offered them safe conduct if they would return to Canada. In response, the Métis demanded complete amnesty, which was unacceptable to the Canadian government. Most of the refugees never returned to Canada, but stayed in exile, where their descendants to this day live in a state of poverty. Too many are still on the economic periphery of White settlements as woodcutters and part time workers on farms and ranches, attempting to supplement their minor sources of income with the hunting of small game. A number were admitted to a reserve and their descendants form a large part of the population of the Rocky Boy Reservation in Montana.

Other Métis took to the current of the Saskatchewan River and a life of trapping in the area around The Pas in Manitoba. Subsequently, many became labourers for the Canadian National Railway and helped build the rail line to Churchill. In the process, they founded a series of small Métis communities along the railway, which are still in existence.

In the year 1885, some families fled to the Mackenzie River area. Later, after the disastrous land scrip debacle in what is now Saskatchewan and Alberta, still others drifted to the Mackenzie basin. A recent detailed study of their descendants was published in 1966, in which the author, Slobodian, remarked:

Among Métis of the southern Mackenzie District, old traditions of the Métis nationality and of the insurrections retain a vitality surprising to the observer.[1]

While some hastened north, others fled to the unsettled areas in the southern part of the North-West Territories. Here, in the Cypress Hills, around Willow Bunch, and in the foothills of the Rockies, where wild game was still abundant, they kept up the old lifestyle for a short period. Even there, where the land was poorly suited for farming, the settlers flocked in within a decade to homestead and the Métis became beggars in their own land.

In the North-West Territories, the Government proceeded to make the same errors regarding the settlement of Métis land claims in 1885 that had been made in Manitoba following the insurrection of 1869-70. A Commission recognized that the land claims of the Métis were justified and, by so doing, they recognized the justice of the complaints leading to the rebellion. Métis children born before July 15, 1870, were given a choice between a money scrip worth $240 or a land scrip that allowed them to choose 240 acres of unoccupied Dominion lands. Heads of families had a similar choice but were limited to $160 or 160 acres. In 1900 the government extended these benefits to children born between 1870 and 1885. Excluded were all those who had received scrip under the Manitoba Act. In 1899, at the signing of Treaty Eight with the Indians of the Athabasca and Peace Rivers, the Métis were given identical grants. In 1921, each Métis of the Mackenzie River District received $240 to extinguish an aboriginal right to the land.

Those Métis who stayed around to collect the scrip (many were afraid to make application) received very little benefit. Living for the present, as most of them did, the majority took the scrip valued at $240 but found that the selling price for a scrip was half the face value, or $120. They sold their scrips hastily and then squandered the money, buying objects of no utility, so that they reduced themselves to misery and became more discouraged and hostile towards White society.[2]

The missionaries, mainly Oblates, advised, but to no avail, against the application of a system which assured the dispossession of the Métis and that did nothing to assist in helping them through a transitional period. Land speculators were active and soon were in possession of vast tracts of fertile land. Merchants deliberately extended credit to Métis beyond their ability to repay and took land scrip to

135

settle the debts.[3] The scrip was such a tempting source of ready cash that many Indians on reserves renounced their treaty status in order to apply for it.

As in Manitoba, there was in Saskatchewan and Alberta a minority that handled the situation with a degree of sophistication and derived some benefit from the possession of land by negotiating the scrip of their children to get cash to purchase livestock and machinery. Of these, however, some did not have the technical agricultural knowledge or experience with livestock to be successful and, in a few years, unable to pay the taxes, they also lost everything. The Métis of St. Lazare, acting on the wise guidance of the priest kept their land, but by 1900 very few still retained possession of it. Today they live in poverty, often squatting on land unwanted by the White farmers who became owners of the farms.

The fact of the matter is that the Métis were asked to work within an economic structure they poorly understood, with obligations and responsibilities to be assumed that their previous lifestyle inhibited. Yet their stage of transition, coupled with a sense of nationhood, was such that it is extremely doubtful if they could have been treated as government wards and kept on reserves as were the Indians. The efforts of the Métis, hindered by the bungling of Ottawa, failed and many became discouraged and dispirited. After so many failures, further attempts at adaptation must have seemed futile, which may account for the apathy and lethargy which began to permeate the Métis people.

Marcel Giraud agrees with Mgr. Grandin that it was an error not to set up a Reserve system for the Métis.[4] Yet the one major effort in this regard proved unsuccessful. Father Therien and Father Lacombe proposed to set up a special area where they could assemble a number of Métis families and prepare them gradually for life as farmers. It was proposed to supply land, livestock, agricultural equipment and tools, together with practical advice and assistance that would bring about a development of agricultural skills. Four townships of land (92,160 acres), named St. Paul des Métis, near the Saddle Lake Indian Reserve in Alberta, were given to a syndicate headed by church personnel. In July 1896, a proclamation announced that Métis in Manitoba and the North-West Territories were eligible to come. Land, equipment, livestock and educational facilities were to be available for the Métis. The government gave the syndicate a grant of

$2,000 and left the rest of the financing to the church. Thirty families came the first year. In 1897, there were fifty families. It was obvious, however, that the Métis were not enthusiastic about agricultural labor. They tilled small fields and raised large gardens, but their most successful efforts were in raising cattle. To the despair of the priests, once their immediate needs were satisfied, the Métis were not concerned about expanding their farms or herds. Yet this was necessary if enough surplus wealth was to be generated to finance schools, churches, roads, and other social amenities that were desired by the priests for the Métis and seemed necessary if a transition to White ways was to be achieved.

Thinking, perhaps, of the successful intermixture of the French-Canadians with the Métis in the Red River Valley after 1870, it was determined to open up the land to a large contingent of French-Canadian settlers. This meant that the syndicate had to be disbanded and that the land subsequently had to be placed under the Homestead Act. By 1910, the legal problems had been solved and resident Métis were given title to the land they occupied. Friction, perhaps because the incoming French-Canadians lacked any understanding of the Métis or possibly because the Métis were relegated to minority status, marred the next few years. Most temporarily met the problem by selling the land to which they now held title, spending the money and either moving away or squatting on unoccupied land nearby. The destitution that developed was blamed on the missionaries who, the Métis felt, had manipulated the situation to benefit the French-Canadians.

In other parts of the country, despite the rapid growth of villages and farms, many Métis reverted to nomadism. Those inhabiting the Mackenzie and Athabasca River basin, Great Slave Lake, Lake la Biche, Lake Ste. Anne, The Pas and similar locations where fur bearing animals and game were still abundant, soon lived by the chase almost entirely. The need to move the entire family as fur, fish and flesh were sought meant that schooling was impossible for the children. The literacy rate of the younger generation declined from even the low level of the parents.

Whether on the prairies or in the woodlands, the government of the country intruded with its laws to restrict yet further the former liberty of the Métis. An increasing number of settlers and the development of farms, which destroyed the natural habitat and increased hunt-

137

ing, brought great pressure upon the wildlife population. In 1890, laws were passed which forbade the hunting of wild fowl such as geese, ducks, partridges and prairie chickens during the mating and nesting season. As necessary as the laws were to preserve the dwindling wild fowl population, it nevertheless caused great hardship to the Métis people, who depended upon wild game for a basic food supply. In 1893, fishing was restricted for similar reasons and worked equally great hardships on the Métis. Many were forced to abandon a life dependent upon hunting, but the only other lifestyle that they had the opportunity to pursue was that of chance employment in agricultural areas. This type of seasonal employment forced a continuation of nomadism and developed a worse poverty-stricken existence. A common sight throughout the West was the Métis family (invariably referred to as Indian, because of the color factor) that wandered across the countryside, with all its worldly possessions piled in a rickety, horse-drawn wagon. They looked for jobs repairing fences in late spring, cut and stacked hay in the summer, stooked and worked on the threshing gangs in the fall, cut wood in the winter and trapped muskrats in the early spring. During all seasons, home was usually an eight foot by twelve foot tent, heated, if at all, by a small tin stove. The raggedly-dressed children were undernourished, rarely attended school and, with their parents, worked unceasingly at trapping and hunting small game in the vicinity of the camp in order to supplement meagre wages or tide the family over from one job to another.

Some were attracted to the new towns in the countryside. On the outskirts of many villages there developed shanty towns which housed the Métis. Houses made of scrap lumber, discarded tin and cardboard, were homes for the poverty-stricken families. They worked when they could and begged or stole food when work was not available. During the prosperous seasons, such as harvesting, the wages earned were often used to buy an escape from the monotonous and depressing poverty in which they lived. The easiest and cheapest escape was through alcohol. With alcohol came quarrels and serious disorders and as a result the Métis became familiar with the interior of jails. Yet the crimes committed were most often those of stealing food and clothing, rarely those of criminals whose trade mark is premeditated crimes. Their crimes were of the moment and usually committed in the face of human need or as a result of the brief excesses of alcohol.

It must be reiterated that there were many Métis who had settled into sedentary life patterns as farmers, small ranchers and fishermen. If they formed a majority in a community, they retained a dignity, pride of race and cohesiveness that kept them from the excesses of the nomads. Unfortunately, some of the families who were being assimilated successfully into predominately White communities began to look with disdain upon their brothers who had not "made it". The nomadic and shanty-town Métis were a nuisance to White communities and an embarrassment to the "successful" Métis. Métis began to cross the color line. They became White. The large number of dark-haired French-Canadians in Manitoba and the West made this easy to do. Possessed of similar physical features to this group (the reader will recall from Chapter Two that many French-Canadians have a strong strain of Indian blood), the progressive Métis were tempted to become French. This was relatively easy to do, especially if they weren't in a French community. The English-speaking half-breeds who were "progressive" took the same tack. They became "Highlanders" or, as the White settlers often referred to them, "Hudson Bay Scotch."

The crossing of a color line was not unique to Canada. In the New England states it was recorded that

> After the Indian wars began, it became unwise to speak of the admixture of Indian blood with the white, and it became popular to blame the straight black hair and swarthy complexions on "Black Highlander" or "Black Irish" ancestry.[5]

Few can be as vindictive as those who wish to appear pure and sinless. So it was with the new "French" and the "Hudson Bay Scotch". Turning on their socially unacceptable brothers with contempt, they were the unceasing critics of the "breeds" and Indians. "Useless misfits in society", "lazy bums", "disgrace to humanity", and other, less complimentary terms were used to direct attention at the "breeds" in such a way that no one would consider associating the speaker with them.

The rate at which the Métis "disappeared" was rapid.

> In 1870, there were 9,830 Métis and half-breeds living in the area incorporated into the Province of Manitoba. If there were no territorial expansion of the Province since then, nor mixed marriages, and if the rate of natural increase of the Métis population had remained constant at 20 per thousand, Manitoba would have a Métis population of over 55,000. Since 1870, however, the Province was enlarged so that additional Métis

settlements became part of Manitoba. Mixed-marriages between Indians, Métis and Whites have also added their sons and daughters to the original Métis population. As a result there may well be between one and two hundred thousand persons in the Province who claim some Indian ancestry.[6]

The last year in which the Dominion Bureau of Statistics counted the Métis separately was in the census of 1941. It showed 8,692 Métis in Manitoba, 8,808 in Alberta and 9,160 in Saskatchewan.

Those who remained as Métis accepted their fate passively. Discouraged, dispirited and poverty-stricken, they entered the twentieth century, which was to bring comfort and wealth to most Canadians, ill prepared to garner their share of the good things Canada had to offer. For two more generations, they were to suffer persecution, humiliation and the denial of the rights enjoyed by other Canadians. As the new century began, the darkest days of the Métis lay ahead.

10

The Forgotten
People

Canada, a vast nation sprawling across the northern half of
North America, moved into the twentieth century with confident exuberance. Railways connected its farthermost points; immigrants
from Europe poured into the open spaces of the West; cities sprouted
across the land and belched forth smoke and concrete in ever increasing amounts. "The twentieth century belongs to us", boasted the
Canadian people and, indeed, the nation did grow, became wealthy
and, in proportion to its population, exerted an undue influence on the
world.

The immigrants, settling the agricultural lands in the West or
working at building the urban centres which catered to the needs of
farmers, had a mental set which assisted in their rapid adaptation to
the western scene. Contrasted with the overcrowded and expensive
lands of Europe, the free land in Canada, or the possibility of owning a
home in the city, was an initial stimulus. Canada was soon found to be
a land where financial success, relative to the country of origin, was
possible for almost anyone willing to work hard, while upward social
mobility for the children was possible through success in the universal
public school system. Working, saving and educating the children
were the multiple points of the immigrant ethic. To this end, most immigrants were willing to be anglicized by the financially and socially
dominant British minority. The dominance of the English language
was largely unquestioned. They were prepared to become "English"
and gave little support to other minority language groups, as evi-

denced in Manitoba when, in 1890, French was abolished as an official language. Willingly, they let their children learn a new symbolism: the Union Jack flying at every school; the singing of "O Canada" and "God Save the King"; the July 1 celebration and the Victoria Day holiday. All these combined to develop in the children a loyalty to Canada, rather than to an "old country". A few groups, mainly of a religious nature, withstood the blandishments of the new society. The Mennonites held out for almost two generations; the Hutterites remain aloof to this day; the Doukhobours split apart and most became an integral part of the new society, as did the second and third generations of other nationalities, such as Icelanders and Ukrainians.

No matter what immigrant group is examined, the majority of its members were hard workers with a future orientation in terms of acquisition of land, money and education. They were people who wished to tame the land, and who judged deer and waterfowl to be a menace to crops and thus enemies to progress. Large houses, well tilled fields and a neatly ordered countryside were evidence of civilization and they considered their role to be precisely that — civilizers of the wild west.

Few of the first citizens of the West, the Indians and Métis, had any role to play in this new, agriculturally-oriented world. The Indian way had been to wander over the prairies and utilize its natural resources for subsistence. The impact of the fur trade changed this orientation but little. Dependent as they became upon metal tools, guns, beads, blankets and alcohol, Indians used the surplus of nature to procure these trade items and gave no thought to agriculture as a means of lessening dependency upon wildlife or the trader. Fortunately for the Indians, the government felt constrained to negotiate treaties and, although shuttled aside, the lands granted them were reserved in tax-free perpetuity. On these small tax free islands, they waited and, although poverty stricken, a population base was developed from which, in the latter half of the twentieth century, some would begin to emerge as people who were confident in themselves. The reserves were a haven in which Indian culture was a cohesive factor and helped the people to evolve slowly and make the necessary adaptations to a new world.

The first half of the twentieth century did not belong to the Métis. They had neither the positive mental set of the immigrant nor a paternalistic government that felt a legal duty to protect, feed and educate them as it did the Indians. The mental set of the Métis was one of hopelessness, and a feeling that failure would be their lot no matter what efforts were expended. The history of the Métis taught that in conflict with Euro-Canadians they would find no success in negotiations, armed conflict or retreat. In a sense, they were a people who had no future and were cheated of the present because the past was filled with pain, hunger, sorrow and despair. The present was thus haunted by the fearful obsession that the past might return. For many of them, the world was a cesspool of unemployment, social ostracism by Whites, spiritual and physical degradation, hunger, long term malnutrition, disease and squalor. Those fortunate enough to escape such evils were the families who had somehow managed to retain land or had established themselves as independent commercial fishermen. Until the 1940's those who had retreated to the wilderness areas did not suffer too greatly. They found it still possible to fish, trap, hunt and generally harvest the natural produce of the countryside. In the worst straits were those who lived in shanty towns on the outskirts of White villages and towns.

The historical groupings of the Métis were only slightly altered: established groups of small farmers, groups who lived off the land in traditional ways, and people living in roughly constructed shacks on "the wrong side of the tracks" in towns and villages. The groups constituted the descendants of the original Métis and half-breeds — descendants of the fur traders, cart men, buffalo hunters, tripmen, farmers, guides and warriors of the plains. They had a heritage and history which they passed on by oral tradition. Even when shunned, despised, downtrodden and belittled, a spark of pride glowed in the hearts of all Métis. Former rulers of the land, indispensable to settlement by the first Europeans, mentors of the Indians, they were men who had lost but, at least, had fought valiantly for their land. These thoughts kept a spark of inner dignity alive and were focused upon the facts and myths surrounding one man: Louis Riel. Many myths developed about Riel: he had escaped and another man was hanged in his place; he was immortal and would return once again to lead the Métis; St. Boniface was not his burial place — the body had been spirited away and buried in a valley known only to the Métis at Willow Bunch, Saskatchewan; the son of Louis Riel (he died as a young man) would take his father's place as a leader and obtain justice for the Métis. The number of tales increased with each succeeding generation.

As time passed, Riel became more saintly, his ideals more perfect, his courage greater and his complete devotion to the Métis cause beyond doubt. It mattered little that only the Métis of Saskatchewan River area had supported Riel in the war of 1885. The insurrection of 1869-70 in Manitoba, the exile of Louis Riel, the rebellion of 1885, the hanging of Riel, these became the *cause celebre* of most Métis, whether of historical or recent origin. Indeed, it did not matter. Riel's ideals were worthy, his actions were honourable and his devotion was for all half-breeds, not just the few he knew personally. His greatest moments were during the trial and his final speech was kept alive in the oral tradition.

> When I came into the North-West in July, 1884, I found the Half-breeds eating rotten pork of the Hudson's Bay Company and getting sick and weak every day. Although a Half-breed I saw that the whites, too were suffering; for they were deprived of responsible government like the rest . . . I remembered the Half-breed meant white and Indian, . . . and I directed my attention to help the Indians, to help the Half-breeds, and to help the whites to the best of my ability.[1]

If he had failed to solve the problem, the Métis considered it a magnificent failure which only increased his greatness. When people said he was insane because of his religious beliefs, the Métis remembered his words at the trial:

> As to religion what is my belief? My insanity, Your Honors, Gentlemen of the Jury, is that I wish to leave Rome aside inasmuch as it is the cause of division between the Catholics and Protestants . . . even if it takes two hundred years to become practical, then after my death . . . my children will shake hands with Protestants of the New World in a friendly manner.[2]

And wasn't this happening whispered the Métis? Were not the churches coming together? Weren't the old hatreds being forgotten by people of all religions? Didn't this prove that Riel was a prophet?

Riel had acted as a man must act when attacked.

> Well, the ministers of this insane and irresponsible Government . . . made up their minds to answer my petition . . . by attempting to jump suddenly upon my people in Saskatchewan . . . When they showed their teeth to devour us, I was ready. That is what is called my crime of high treason . . .[3]

These were the remembered words. These were some of the thoughts kept alive within Métis people wherever destiny led them. These were the sparks that would one day ignite another generation of

Métis to rally once more into organized bodies, though the times would demand that the bodies be political rather than military. This, then, was the essence of the spirit hidden deep within the Métis people, as they eked out a miserable existence in the first half of the twentieth century.

Scattered across Canada from Newfoundland to the Queen Charlotte Islands were people of mixed-blood who knew themselves and were known by their neighbors as breeds, half-breeds, Métis and mulligan stew Canadians. Some of these mixed-bloods lived on the fringes of Indian Reserves. Not allowed by law to live on the reserve, but usually related by marriage to the Indians, these Métis were culturally like the reserve residents. The old Indian beliefs, lifestyles and customs were kept alive by frequent contact with relatives on the reserves. Because of this, they needed the same assistance in education, health and welfare as Indians, but were not served by the Federal Government through its Indian Affairs Branch because they were not legally Indians, as defined by the Indian Act.[4] Often, these essential services were not available from the provincial governments because of the isolated nature of the Métis communities on the fringes of reserves. The children frequently attended the reserve school when there was room and were excluded when the schools became crowded. Lacking any assistance from government, housing was usually poor. There was no money for economic development and medical services were intermittent. Nevertheless, all was not negative, for most Métis retained both vigor and initiative because of this state of neglect. They had to fend for themselves and rarely developed the passive dependency characteristic of so many of the Indian residents of reserves.

An unknown number, perhaps approximating the number of those on the outskirts of reserves, lived on the fringes of White settlements. These were inhabitants of the notorious Shanty Towns which were liberally sprinkled across Canada. Usually, the Shanty Town inhabitants were nomadic in that they moved from rural areas to towns and back again, according to the employment opportunities available. The Shanty Towns, rather than the inhabitants, were permanent. Opportunities for casual employment lured the residents from one place to another. The poor standards of housing, law enforcement problems, racial discrimination, lack of attendance at school and a nomadic existence made them a group of which Canadians were very much aware. They were visible as those in isolation were not. Their visibility brought the negative attitudes of the White communities into focus upon them with disastrous results for all Métis.

> People surrounded by the inefficiency and disorder are not likely to develop the type of ambition and pride which would lead them to achieve a higher standard of living. They tend to believe that efforts for betterment of self and family are not likely to succeed. In order to find some happiness, the fringe dweller must develop a philosophy of life suitable to his condition which would include an acceptance of his condition as necessary under the circumstances and the search for happiness in more easily attainable goals.
>
> The existence of fringe settlements inhabited primarily by one ethnic group leads the public to think that most of the members of that ethnic group live under marginal conditions. Only 10 percent of the Métis population live on the fringe of white settlements while another 10 percent live on the fringe of reserves. More than 75 percent of the Métis do not live on fringe settlements, yet many Manitobans think of them as people who do. Their concept of what a Métis home looks like is taken from fringe settlements.[5]

There were, of course, many predominantly Métis communities. Those mentioned in previous chapters largely retained their Métis inhabitants. Such communities were found in agricultural areas; along lakes and rivers where commercial fishing was possible; on the edge of wilderness areas where traplines were feasible; close to railways and in forested areas where employment in lumber camps and saw mills was possible. Here, also, the housing was substandard, educational opportunities were limited and, since work was available only sporadically, the people lived in harsh poverty. Although poverty-stricken, it was within these communities that the Métis identity remained strong. This sense of identity contributed to their adjustment for group solidarity and kept alive the social sanctions that are so important in community control. The social and cultural disintegration found in fringe communities was, fortunately, lacking in predominantly Métis settlements. Cultural assimilation to White ways was slow and thus handled without undue stress. From these stable communities were to come many of the leaders of the Métis in the decades of the 1960's and 1970's.

The Métis who adapted most successfully were those living in White communities. Educated estimates placed this group at well over half the Métis in Canada. Growing up in White communities, attending White schools, learning patterns of work acceptable to the Whites, the first generation tended to be bicultural. The second and third generations were unicultural and that culture was Euro-Canadian. They were culturally and educationally assimilated. These Métis naturally intermarried with White men and women and their visibility lessened with each succeeding generation. Many of them easily dropped any reference to an Indian background and crossed the color line. Others became what is often referred to as "historical" Métis. They were culturally Euro-Canadian but aware and proud of both the Indian background and the history of their half-breed ancestors. These historical Métis were located largely in the southern parts of the three prairie provinces and were descendants of the Red River half-breeds who had scattered across the West and settled into an agricultural or urban life. The Métis kept their history alive through the organization, *L'union métisse St. Joseph* which was founded in 1887 and is still active, now bearing the name *L'union nationale métisse St. Joseph de Manitoba.* Its activities were directed towards the French-speaking half-breeds and, as French was used almost exclusively in its assemblies, it tended to exclude those Métis who spoke English or had acculturated towards various Indian tribes. *L'union métisse* is of considerable significance to its members, for people who are unaware of, or cannot accept, their past, often have serious personality conflicts — especially if, as individuals, they are visible to the general public because of skin color, name or accent.

These historical Métis, both French and English, were largely acculturated to either English or French-Canadians. They were educated, economically self sufficient and had a wealth of expertise which, if it had been available to the less fortunate Métis, would have been of considerable assistance to the latter. Unfortunately, some historical Métis were contemptuous of their less fortunate brothers and stayed as far away from them and their problems as possible.

Across Canada, a basic problem of the unacculturated Métis was economic. Historical work styles did not change easily to those unremitting 8:00 a.m. to 5:00 p.m. types of labor that were now central to the work ethic. Adaptation was difficult, for in many communities even the opportunity for steady employment was completely lacking. The Métis fell into the rhythm of seasonal employment, which ill prepared them for transition to an urban lifestyle that would become predominant in Canada. Some became seasonal workers in logging camps across Canada. Those that lived beside lakes were employed during fishing seasons. Others trapped, guided tourists in search of fish and game or worked on construction projects. In certain areas, seasonal types of independent work were still available. The digging of seneca root, the extract of which is used in making cough drops and syrups, supplemented other income. Small native fruits, such as blueberries, saskatoons and strawberries, were picked during July and August. In certain areas of Ontario and Manitoba, the harvesting of wild rice was a source of income during the fall. Frogs were caught during the summer for shipment to either restaurants or zoological laboratories. Having made a living from these types of seasonal work, the Métis found themselves even more disadvantaged when mechanization gradually replaced manpower in industry. The Métis found that they had skills that were not marketable in the rapidly developing industrial world. Their level of education was so low that industry could not train them for other tasks without first upgrading their academic skills; this was a task that industry was not prepared to undertake. Time, tribulation and sorrow would overcome many of the social and cultural problems, but only education would give them access to well-paying jobs in the industrial world.

In compiling statistics concerning educational achievement among the Métis of Manitoba, Lagasse found that in 1959,

> 23 percent of the Métis interviewed in rural Manitoba had received no education whatever. Questions about the schooling which their parents had received showed that 69 percent had never been to school.[6]

Gradual improvement was apparent, though to no significant level.

Average School Leaving Grade for the Métis in Manitoba[7]

Age Group	Average School Leaving Grade
50-59	2.55
40-49	2.93
30-39	3.80
20-29	5.37

It can be assumed that these statistics for Manitoba reflect the entire Canadian situation, since each province was plagued with similar educational problems in the isolated Indian and Métis schools. Inadequate facilities and overcrowded classrooms, staffed by untrained and underpaid teachers, were common. Many Métis communities in isolated areas had no schools at all and in those schools that did exist the highest grade offered was usually grade eight.

Overcrowded, poorly heated homes were a major determinant of the health of Métis children.

Many of the homes visited were overcrowded. At Birch River, 15 persons were living in a two room shack 12' x 24'. There was not enough bedspace for more than six. At Wabowden, a family group of 19 persons lived in three small rooms. A one room, 14' x 20', log house in another community housed a couple and their seven children. Three small boys slept on the floor, a baby swung from the ceiling in a hammock, the parents slept in a standard double bed and three teenage girls (the oldest 18 years old) slept in a smaller bed at the foot of the parents' bed.[8]

Inadequate diet, lack of parental understanding of what education might do for children, discrimination against Métis in some schools, coupled with poverty which forced children to become wage earners at the earliest possible age, combined to keep the educational level low.

It seemed to many Métis people that the only way to break the cycle of poverty and lack of educational opportunities was to move to White communities. The attitudes of some communities were extremely negative, as indicated by the following report of a rural municipal council published in a local weekly newspaper:

It was brought to the attention of Council that several treaty and non-treaty (Métis) Indians, with large families, are now moving into the village, most of them being indigents and trying to establish residence here. The Council decided to have an inspection made at once of their homes and surroundings and if unsuitable or liable to be on relief, to have their homes condemned and action taken to have them removed from the village.[9]

A varied selection of quotations will indicate the barriers raised against Métis people who wished to move from Shanty Town to the main part of the community:

We probably have several Métis or Half-Breed families as residents but we have only had a few occasions where relief had been a problem. These families were usually employed as labourers on dairy farms and we endeavour to have them return to the area from which they migrated.[10]

*　　　*　　　*

A municipal official confessed that names of Métis families likely to become indigent had not been included on a Provincial electoral list 'for fear they believe that they have earned residence in our town and request financial assistance.'[11]

There were, however, people in every community who raised objections to the treatment received by Métis.

It is really fantastic and unbelievable that here in Manitoba in 1958, it is quite right and acceptable that we should chase a human being and his family out of town simply because through no fault of his own, all his forebearers were born in this land.[12]

Any excuse was used to keep them out of school. It was not felt necessary to have a medical certificate when Métis children were involved.

Moved by B.   , seconded by H.   that the McKay children not be allowed to attend school as this half-breed family is suspected of having tuberculosis.

Carried.[13]

The following excerpt from a study concerning prejudice towards Indians and Métis indicates the most biased occupational classes.

Frequency of Prejudiced Responses by Occupational Class[14]

	Percent
Professional etc.	4.4
Farmers, etc.	6.0
Proprietors, managers, etc.	10.4
Clerical, sales, etc.	4.5
Craftsmen, foremen, etc.	23.8
Operative, etc.	6.0
Protective Service	3.0
Service Workers	3.0
Laborers	30.0
Unemployed	1.5
Retired	7.5

The three highest percentages pertain to laborers (30.0), craftsmen, foremen (23.8), proprietors, managers (10.4). These were the people who would hire and/or work beside the Métis. Even if the Métis were hired, the substantial minority prejudiced against him would make social and working conditions very uncomfortable. Deeply prejudiced foremen and managers would hire Métis only as a last resort and dismiss them at the first opportunity.

The three prairie provinces of Manitoba, Saskatchewan and Alberta contained the largest numbers of Métis and the provincial governments made a number of attempts to ease the problems. Special projects were set up to test new ideas and, although some were successful, governments rarely invested sufficient money to extend the programs.

Alberta attempted to help the Métis become farmers by instituting a system of land holding that was a variation of the Indian reserve idea. In 1938, under the Métis Population Betterment Act, Alberta set aside 1,300,000 acres of provincial lands, located in seven different areas, for the use of the Métis. Within these settlements, community projects such as lumbering, fishing and farming were set up, with all profits being placed in a Métis Trust Fund. The money in the fund was then used to establish and improve educational and health services. The settlement scheme was initially successful and, by 1955, contained over 2000 Métis people. Unfortunately the project was found to be too costly to extend to the general Métis population. Its more recent lack of success can be attributed to the increasing difficulties experienced by all small business ventures that are in competition with the well funded, efficient, largely mechanized corporations which are taking over primary industries, such as pulp and paper, fish and even farms.

Saskatchewan attempted a similar scheme at Green Lake in 1946. There, a number of Métis were given ownership of agricultural land, assisted in building houses, helped to clear the land of trees and loaned money to purchase seed, stock and farm equipment. The success of this venture led to the setting up of the Lacerte Co-operative Farm at Willow Bunch, which developed large market gardens and a small livestock industry. Once again, a fairly successful project proved too costly to be extended.

The government of Saskatchewan made an effort to assist the Métis trappers and hunters of the north when two events threatened their established lifestyle. One event which had repercussions in all northern areas across Canada was the development of artificial furs, which were as pleasing and warm as natural furs, but much cheaper. Fur prices declined to a point where a trapper could no longer earn a living. Parallel to this problem was a second one: the rapidly growing population in northern areas, which resulted in a depletion of wildlife from excessive hunting.

A Fur Marketing Service was established by Saskatchewan in 1945, as a non-profit Crown Corporation. Its main purpose was to conserve the still valuable beaver and muskrat populations by limiting the number that could be trapped. In an attempt to increase the money earned by trappers, all furs were purchased by the Fur Marketing Service. As the independent fur traders could no longer buy the furs, they were reluctant to "grubstake", or advance credit for the supplies and equipment that the trapper needed, so that he was unable to venture very far into the wilderness to trap. Yet it was in the more remote areas that the furs were most abundant. Although initiated with the best of intentions, the government plan back-fired and the Métis were left poorer than ever.

The Block Conservation System was an attempt to assign specific trapping areas to individuals. The intention was to have each man so regulate his trapping of beaver and muskrat that the population would remain constant. Each block had a small settlement at its core, where the trappers and their families would live. Schools were built to serve the children. Small lots of land were granted to each family and gardening was encouraged. Unfortunately, the shacks of the Métis were unsuited to the storage of vegetables over the winter and, indeed, the people had not developed a liking for any vegetables other than the potato. The increasing population, combined with the limited number of trapping areas, soon created a situation in which a large number of families in each settlement were living on welfare. This was accompanied by increased consumption of alcohol and an upsurge in the crime rate, as well as a greater number of broken homes.

In 1940, the Manitoba Government instituted a Registered Traplines program. Groups or individuals were given exclusive rights to trap in a certain defined and registered area. Thus, it was to a trapper's advantage to trap wisely and conserve the various fur-bearing animals. Without interfering with traditional buying and selling practices, this system worked reasonably well and to the advantage of the Métis.

In both Saskatchewan and Manitoba, the governments expended considerable effort and money in assisting Métis and Indian people to form co-operatives — both producer and consumer types. Stores, fish, wild rice, fur and pulpwood were types of co-operatives commonly formed. Although some of these were unsuccessful in financial terms, they succeeded in giving Métis people an insight into the complexities of business, laws and government bureaucracies, as well as helping them learn the verbal skills necessary in order to work in formal situations.

Government efforts to assist the Métis across Canada were characterized more often by failure than by success. The dominant society developed projects to assist certain groups of Métis but the projects assumed that the Métis shared the same aspirations and values as the middle class White people who served as leaders. Such efforts were well intentioned but often unsuccessful.

Following the Second World War, the mechanization of almost every aspect of Canadian life proceeded at a rapid pace. Farms became larger and the surplus population moved to the cities.

Pulpwood operations increased production, while decreasing the number of workers employed. Registered traplines and similar schemes limited the number of men involved in trapping, while an increasing demand for fish, coupled with more efficient fishing equipment, strained the capacity of the lakes. To conserve the fish, governments began to regulate the catch, as well as to limit the number of commercial fishing licenses issued. Lack of employment in rural and isolated areas, coupled with the intense prejudice and blatant discrimination against the Métis in small rural villages and towns, caused those who desired to break the cycle of poverty to move to large urban centers. There, amongst vast populations, the Métis hoped to find a haven.

While unemployment, prejudice and discrimination may be considered rural "push" factors, urban centres contained many "pull" factors that acted as a lure to Métis people. Opportunities for employment were greater, but to the Métis it was undoubtedly the material factors which exerted considerable "pull". Running water, indoor toilets, automatic heat, relative freedom from insects, greater security in terms of welfare, closeness to medical aid, movies, varied recreational facilities and the possibility of becoming financially successful were all great attractions. The vigor, variety and stimulation of city life not only drew the Métis, but held them.

Because of the difficulty of identification of Métis, no data have been gathered concerning the numbers in Canada's cities. Educated estimates have been made by various research groups and social service agencies. Estimates for three major cities are as follows:

	1945	1960
Vancouver	500	4000
Winnipeg	200*	6000*
Toronto	700	6800

*excluding the "historical" mixed-bloods who were fully acculturated.

After 1960, the steady influx became a flood and estimates for Winnipeg placed its Métis population at 11,000 in 1965. One can assume a similar increase in other cities.

Entering the cities without marketable skills, most Métis were forced to earn a living by working as unskilled laborers. By so doing, most earned the minimum wage and were frequently unemployed, for such work usually was of an outdoor nature that was influenced by weather conditions.

Low wages forced many into the cheapest houses in the dilapidated areas of the cities. In such depressing conditions, and with no recourse but to accept welfare when unemployed, they were again victims of prejudice and discrimination. The larger society felt uncomfortable with Métis in its midst and often rebuffed them when they sought help, friendship and understanding.

Once again, no exact figures are available to indicate what percentages were successful or unsuccessful.

> Native people estimate that perhaps 15-20% of those migrating to the city encounter serious problems. Possibly 30-35% encounter some problems but receive help from Friendship Centres or various social agencies and ultimately become adjusted to city life. The other 50% experience few difficulties and . . . are successful and relatively happy in the city.[15]

In response to the problem of Indian and Métis in the cities, there developed new institutions known as Friendship Centers. Most cities and large towns had such a center, usually organized in the first instance by concerned White persons in cooperation with Indians and Métis. Such centers served as places where people could socialize with friends, as well as receive information about jobs, housing, legal aid and emergency financial help. Friendship Centers organized recreational and cultural activities in addition to assisting special groups, such as Alcoholics Anonymous. The extreme value of these services was acknowledged by ever-increasing financial grants given them by federal, provincial and municipal governments.

At this point it is necessary to introduce another element into the complexity of the Métis story. There has always been a clause in the Indian Act that allowed Indians to "enfranchise" themselves. Enfranchisement refers to a legal process by which an Indian gives up all rights and privileges to which he is entitled under the Indian Act. In so doing, he ceases to have the right to live on a reserve and must sell to other Indians whatever reserve property he may own. When this step has been taken, he must pay income tax, finance the education of his children, pay his own medical, hospital and drug bills and lose special hunting and trapping privileges. In short, he accepts the responsibilities of a Canadian citizen and loses the special status of an Indian. A male or female may take this action freely and willingly, but if an Indian woman marries a White man she is automatically enfranchised.

Through enfranchisement, many Indians become "non-status" Indians. When surveys by social researchers or census takers were made, the "enfranchised" people could no longer claim to be Indian. Many chose to list themselves as Métis rather than as something else. Large numbers of these people, having severed their legal ties with the reserves, sought a new life in the cities. For many, this move created an identity crisis. Suddenly, they wished to return to a traditional Indian culture, not as it was on the reserve, but as they thought it might have been three or four generations ago. Dance clubs sprang up. Cree, Sioux, Ojibway, Mohawk, Micmac, Assiniboine — all the different Indians found in an urban center — combined to form "cultural" groups. They traded ideas about dance steps, costumes and songs. The resultant mixture of tribal cultures with modern White ways would have astounded an Indian of a century ago. But it served its purpose in helping these people manufacture a needed identity. Having regained a "cultural" Indian identity, they discovered that they were still rejected by the Indian organizations because they weren't legally Indian. To compensate, many joined and worked within the Métis groups or formed Métis and non-status Indian associations. Their presence within the Métis associations was to be a source of dissension and conflict for these organizations in the future.

In the decades of the fifties and sixties, there occurred a remarkable development, first in Manitoba, and later in other provinces. A new approach by government, under the general title of community development, was put into practice. Community Development Programs attempted to assist communities through planned stages of development. The first stage was to help people in the community develop an awareness of their needs. When these needs had been identified, the Community Development Worker used his expertise to help the people to become familiar with the possibilities within their reach and the resources available to them. If the people rejected the need of a program to solve a particular problem, the Community Development Worker helped them identify other problems which they might be more ready to consider. If a problem was identified and a project developed in an attempt to solve it, the Community Development Worker facilitated the efforts of the people to understand the complexities of the various government departments with which they had to deal. "Facilitator" is a term which accurately described a Community Development Worker. He facilitated the efforts of a community to help itself and, in the process, the leadership potential of the people was developed.

If the Métis communities that undertook such programs were surveyed, the majority of members would likely say that Community Development was a waste of time and money. Yet the objective observer would have to quarrel with that judgment. Districts with such programs may have gained little in material benefits, but a different attitude was apparent. The people were no longer as apathetic about life and many had developed a spirit of critical inquiry. They had learned to verbalize in groups and reach decisions. A sense of political awareness characterized them, while apathy and indifference were less marked. In many communities, a revolution of the mind and spirit seemed evident, not to the community itself, but to the outside observer. This new spirit was to manifest itself in the local, provincial and federal organizations that the Métis began to form.

ADAM CUTHAND
First president of a national organization of Métis (Canadian Métis Society, 1968).

11

The Development of
Political Organizations

The Métis continued to be a disadvantaged group, socially, economically and politically. These disadvantages were interrelated. Generally, groups that are poor are held in low social esteem by the community and tend to lack political influence. Such groups have attempted to solve their problems in various ways, but the greatest success has been achieved by those who have been able to develop cohesive organizations.

The role of such organizations has been to work on behalf of the people to:

1. identify problems;
2. establish an order of priority for the solution of problems at a provincial and national level;
3. develop an awareness and understanding of problems among governments and influential citizens' groups;
4. gain funding and government action to solve or alleviate the problems; and
5. exert continuing pressure upon governments to meet the needs of the group.

Governments always have been subject to more demands than it is possible to meet. No government can attend to more than a small percentage of the requests for funds, use of personnel, and development of new programs. The priorities that governments set are only partially determined by fairness, objectivity or the wise deployment of funds and personnel. Priorities frequently reflect issues that a government can not ignore if it wishes to be re-elected. Usually, the disadvantaged are numerically small and thus are unable to influence a government by direct votes and are forced to bring their problems to public attention and to hope that widespread interest can be created which, in turn, will be reflected at the polls. Only if the issue catches the public fancy will this come about.

In considering the Métis people, it is obvious that history did not create a positive image of them in the minds of Whites. White people thought of the Métis as a rather primitive type of man and, although half-breed was originally a useful and descriptive term, it soon became one of scorn and derision. People perceived the half-breeds as the "illegitimate children of the fur trade", for school texts and novels rarely portrayed the full range of social relationships that had created them. Most people vaguely remembered something to the effect that Indians in Western Canada were colorful and primitive, but not belligerent. The Métis were remembered for the role they played in the Battle of Seven Oaks, the 1870 Insurrection in Manitoba and the 1885 Rebellion in Saskatchewan. When the settlers surged into the West, the Indians were tucked away neatly on reserves and school history books left the impression that they were a happy people contentedly living out their lives under government supervision. Less desirable were the "breeds", who were depicted as roaming the countryside, sometimes working, sometimes stealing, but a nuisance at all times.

Many early settlers experienced pangs of conscience as they tilled the land that had formerly been the preserve of the Métis. To account for the growing wealth of the settler and the abject poverty of the Métis, the Whites created the myth of the lazy half-breed, for such a myth helped salve the conscience. The settlers persuaded themselves that, if the Métis had worked, they could have been well-off also. If the half-breed had been a good citizen and had not rebelled, he would not have experienced difficulties. The three myths of "primitive", "lazy", and "rebel" were so firmly implanted in the mind of the public that it was not receptive to the first efforts of the Métis organizations to tell a different story to the public. It was with this negative image that the Métis first had to struggle.

As the Second World War ended, a dramatic change occurred in relationships between the White and non-White peoples of the world. Western colonialism began to crumble and the colored people struggled to regain control of their destinies. The changing world scene forced the Canadian public to reconsider its attitudes towards minority colored groups at home. The struggles of the Negroes in the United States, in particular, aroused the sympathies of most Canadians, at the same time leading them to wonder about the treatment of Canadian minorities. The result was that, from 1960 onwards, the Canadian public became obsessed with its most vocal minority, the Indians. There was no end to television documentaries exposing the poverty common to the reserves. Books, pamphlets, newspapers and films concerning Indians flooded the market and the Indian Affairs Branch became the favorite whipping boy of the Canadian public. Every and any problem concerning Indians was laid at its door. If the civil servants were only more dedicated, went the lament, Indians wouldn't have problems. When the fad of blaming Indian Affairs personnel became less popular, the Federal Government was attacked on both financial and legal fronts. The public demanded greater expenditures on Indians, larger grants to Indian Bands and an end to legal discrimination in terms of the right to vote, service on juries, local control by bands and a long list of related items. The public were concerned in a general way, without understanding the complexity of the problem, and demanded that instant, simple solutions be devised. With its usual good intentions, the public wished to categorize its citizens of native ancestry in an equally simplistic way. If the skin were brown, the person was an Indian. The legal aspects of patrilineal descent, treaty, registered and non-status Indians and the laws of genetics were details too complex for the average, uninformed citizen to understand. A brown skin equalled Indian and everyone wanted to be his friend and protector. Métis people found, to their sorrow, that when they presented their unique problems, the general public and many government officials translated the requests into programs and grants designed to help the Indians. The harder the Métis worked, the more attention Indians received. This, then, was the social setting in which mixed-bloods attempted to develop their modern organizations.

Métis efforts to organize themselves had historically centered around a crisis and, when this had passed, the organization dissolved. In 1815-16, they organized under Cuthbert Grant to keep the pemmican trade open to all. In 1849, the focus was the Sayer trial and the attempt to free the fur trade from the monopoly of the Hudson's Bay Company. They rallied again in 1869-70 in order to secure traditional land rights, while the last stand of Métis people to preserve their lands took place in 1885. In each instance the organizational model used was comparable to that developed for the buffalo hunt and, when the particular incident had passed, the organization disbanded as had the buffalo hunters.

The first and most permanent Métis organization was historically, rather than politically, oriented. In 1887, *L'union métisse St. Joseph* was organized. Its primary aims were of a cultural and social nature. Local units of the association operated in small communities and, usually with the leadership and support of the Church, held dances, socials and picnics. Such activities helped these Métis, predominantly French-speaking and Roman Catholic, to maintain an identity which stood them in good stead. *L'union métisse* appointed a history committee whose purpose was to defend the role of the Métis in the insurrection of 1869-70 and the rebellion of 1884-85. The role of the organization is still primarily historical. It does not concern itself with the economic problems of its members and social activities are restricted to an annual conference.

In various small communities, associations of Métis had been formed in response to a local crisis or social need, but these rarely lasted very long. Not until 1931 was there developed another provincial organization, when, on the west coast, a Native Brotherhood of British Columbia began serving as a very effective agent in retaining fishing and timber rights for half-breeds and Indians. Membership was open to all persons of native ancestry. The Métis of Saskatchewan formed an association in 1937, but geographical distance combined with lack of money to make it weak and ineffective in its first decades.

The most significant factor in assisting both Métis and Indian people to organize was the Community Welfare Planning Council of Greater Winnipeg. In response to concern evidenced by some White people in Manitoba, the Council sponsored an Indian and Métis conference in 1954 and, in each succeeding year, a similar conference was held. Soon most Indian reserves and Métis communities were sending delegates, whose travelling expenses were heavily subsidized by the Welfare Planning Council. The purposes of the meetings were twofold: to focus attention on the needs of the people of native ancestry and to provide them with a platform from which to suggest ways of resolving social and economic problems. The annual meetings were extremely successful and soon delegates from other provinces were attending. At the 1960 meeting, a group of Indian and Métis people decided to hold

164

a separate conference with a view to forming a national organization. As a result, the National Indian Council was formed in 1961 at Regina, Saskatchewan. Membership was restricted to persons of native ancestry and the Council came to be dominated by Métis and Indian people who were successful urban dwellers. This sophisticated group brought to the Council a knowledge of bureaucracies and a political awareness that helped to establish a new principle, for they persuaded the federal government to pay annual grants to the National Indian Council. The establishment of that precedent was to pave the way for federal funding of succeeding national and provincial organizations. Of importance, also, was the work of the Council in sponsoring travelling art exhibits, princess pageants and the Indian pavilion at Expo '67. These activities helped to modify the basically negative image of native peoples held by many Canadians.

The National Indian Council, lacking large sums of money, was restricted to the role of explaining the plight of native people. As no change at the provincial and community levels resulted from its work, many persons of native ancestry regarded the Council with suspicion. It did, however, prove to be a good training ground for future leaders and many of its executive members helped form and later led provincial organizations. In 1968, the organization decided to dissolve itself in order to form the National Indian Brotherhood and the Canadian Métis Society. Such a division pleased most of the registered Indians and the Métis. It did, however, leave the enfranchised or non-status Indians without an organization to represent them. Rejected by the registered Indians, the non-status Indians turned, with a degree of reluctance, to the Métis Society and were, with equal reluctance, accepted as members.

The Indian-Eskimo Association was formed in 1960. It was non-sectarian, non-political, and dedicated to the cause of Canada's native people. Basically, it was an education and research oriented organization with membership open to all Canadians and was, quite naturally, dominated by White people. It published bulletins, submitted briefs to governments, organized conferences, engaged in research and developed provincial branches of the parent body. Many Canadian people came to believe, however, that the organization was the spokesman for native people. This disturbed Indian and Métis organizations and they persuaded the Indian-Eskimo Association to change its name, in 1972, to the Canadian Association in Support of

Native Peoples (C.A.S.N.P.). Although the principle of support of native persons was sound, certain provincial branches of C.A.S.N.P. were allegedly led by members who opposed the policies of the provincial native organizations. In some cases, civil servants became leaders in the C.A.S.N.P. at the provincial level and incurred the anger of native organizations by allegedly using their executive positions to further the aims of the provincial governments. As a result of these and related problems, the National Indian Brotherhood withdrew its support of the C.A.S.N.P. in 1972. A number of the provincial Métis Associations have been considering such action but, to date, none have formally done so. Harold Cardinal, one of the most articulate Indian leaders, stated in 1969 that the Indian-Eskimo Association was more of a hindrance than a help to the development of strong native organizations, because it drew money from both government and business that could be used more effectively by Indian and Métis groups.[2] Professor Symons, C.A.S.N.P. President in 1972, was reported to have said: "We support native people — not native organizations."[3] The split between native organizations and an association dominated by well intentioned White people shows no sign of being healed. If the present situation continues, it will be regrettable. The C.A.S.N.P. has access to expertise that is, at this moment, not readily available to the native organizations, while its effectiveness will be minimized without Indian and Métis support.

The National Métis Society, founded in 1968, elected as its first president Dr. Adam Cuthand, who had been instrumental in organizing the Manitoba Métis Foundation and also served as its first president. A lack of funds was only one of the problems faced by the Canadian Métis Society. It was an artifical creature encouraged by the Indian-Eskimo Association, did not arise from expressed needs of the existing provincial associations and, therefore, lacked a firm base of support. It was all head and no body. Despite this, it limped along until a new organization developed from the expressed needs of the rapidly growing provincial associations.

On November 16, 1970, the leaders of the Métis Associations of Manitoba, Saskatchewan and Alberta met with the British Columbia Association of Non-Status Indians in Victoria. At the meeting, the leaders agreed to form a national organization. A series of subsequent meetings were held and, in April, 1971, the Native Council of Canada was officially launched and a national office established in Ottawa.

PROVINCIAL MÉTIS AND NON-STATUS INDIAN ASSOCIATIONS

Name	Date Founded	Number of Locals	Priorities
British Columbia Association of Non-Status Indians	1969	60	1 housing 2 education 3 employment 4 human rights
Métis Association of Alberta	1961	75	1 land tenure 2 housing 3 education 4 economic development
Métis Society of Saskatchewan	1937	135	1 housing 2 welfare 3 education 4 health
Manitoba Métis Federation	1967	97	1 housing 2 economic development 3 employment 4 education
L'union national métisse St. Joseph de Manitoba	1887		1 historical
Ontario Métis and Non-Status Indian Assoc.	1971	39	1 housing 2 land 3 economic development 4 employment
Laurentian Alliance of Métis and Non-Status Indians	1972	21	1 housing 2 education 3 health & welfare 4 employment
Métis and Non-Status Native Association of the North West Territories	1972		
New Brunswick Association of Non-Status Indians	1972		information not available
Union of Nova Scotia	1972		
Native Associations of Newfoundland/Labrador	1973		

The provincial presidents and vice-presidents formed the board of directors. The executive officers to date have been:

	1971	1972
President	A. E. Belcourt (Alberta)	A. E. Belcourt (Alta.)
Vice-President	J. Sinclair (Sask.)	Y. Dumont (Man.)
Secretary-Treasurer	A. Spence (Man.)	G. Gabert (B.C.)

The Native Council of Canada was intended to act as the group agent in Ottawa and attempt to secure for individual provinces and territories the funding of programs designed to meet local needs. In broad terms, it sought to achieve full native participation in the mainstream of Canada's social, cultural and economic life.[4]

The difficult problem of defining precisely who might be a member was solved by agreeing upon rather exact definitions of "Métis" and "non-status Indian."

> Métis . . . Mixed blood between Indian and other; also "half-breed" and "breed". In the prairie provinces and N. W. Ontario, anyone of Indian ancestry who is not under the Indian Act.
> Non-Status Indian . . . Person of Indian ancestry who has lost Indian status through enfranchisement, marriage or who was refused Indian status by the federal agency.[5]

The union of Métis and non-status Indians in one organization has not proved as yet, to be a satisfactory marriage, for the two groups are uneasy bedfellows. Most of the Métis people of southern Quebec, western Ontario, the three prairie provinces and parts of the North West Territories and the Yukon are a unique group. Their history and heritage is rooted in the first periods of White-Indian contact. Historically, the Métis have been a major determinant in the westward expansion of Canada and, as a people who struggled to establish a New Nation, they occupy an important place in Canadian history. That they lost was unfortunate. The persecution and hardship endured following their defeat was a bitter tragedy. Yet, despite this, few Métis harbor hatred or even bitterness. Whom would they hate? They are of both the White and Indian world. Attacks on either would be foolish, as well as futile. Most Métis seek to integrate fully into the mainstream of society. Their individualistic nature, however, is such that they tolerate a variety of objectives. If a Métis wishes to assimilate and disappear into White society, it is his privilege to do so and, though his loss to the group may be lamented, no criticism will be directed at him. Unlike many other minority groups, the Métis are basically non-conformist. They see themselves not as Indians or Whites, but as a unique people free to choose to identify with whichever group they desire. Indians claim to be a people with special rights and privileges. Most Métis claim only to be people with special problems.

Angus Spence, President of the Manitoba Métis Federation, said:

> "The Métis people in Manitoba are the most forgotten people in the civilized world. We are told we don't exist. They say, you know, where are they? how many are there? etc. etc. I can assure you we do exist, and this is the reason I am here. We have been isolated from the rest of society. All we are doing is knocking on the door trying to get in.
> The total picture is to rehabilitate an unfortunate people into the mainstream of society. As far as I'm concerned, that is the objective. Once that objective is reached and our people are fitting into the mainstream of society on an equal plane our objective will have been achieved and we can dispense with the Manitoba Métis Federation."[6]

Although not all Métis would agree completely with Angus Spence, it is clear that the great majority do. Most do not want tax free reserves, free education, free medical care and yearly gifts from the Government of Canada. They want employment that will give them a decent wage with which they can raise their families, buy homes and allow them to accept the responsibility and privilege of paying taxes, as does every other Canadian. They want, in short, a place of equality in the economic and social life of Canadian society.

The non-status Indians are quite different and may be divided into three basic categories. One is composed of Indians who are "enfranchised". They, or their fathers, sold the special status they once had as Indians and, in return for a sum of money paid to them by government, became ordinary Canadians. Many who did so continued to live on a reserve and the children grew up as Indians — culturally, but not legally. Still others were illegitimate children, suspected by an Indian band to have a non-Indian father. The band had the privilege of not granting membership to such children and exercised it in many instances. Still other non-status Indians became so because an Indian woman married a White man and automatically lost her status. If widowed or deserted by her husband, the woman often returned to live with relatives on the reserve, but Indian status could never be regained. Large numbers of non-status Indians throughout Canada fit one of these categories. In 1961 there were 2,606 non-status Indians living on reserves.

1210 — women of Indian origin who had lost their Indian status through marriage or enfranchisement, and their non-Indian children . . .
511 — children of unmarried Indian mothers who had been declared not entitled to be registered as Indians on account of non-Indian paternity; and non-Indian children who became Indians in marriage.
288 — non-Indian children adopted or otherwise cared for by Indians.
597 — adult non-Indians and non-Indian children of such persons, other than those described in other categories . . .[7]

Still larger numbers live off the reserves in Métis communities or in urban areas. These people, physically and spiritually, often yearn to return to the protective womb of the reserve, where friendship and security are more readily available.

The second category of non-status Indians consists of those, often young people, who never developed an identity as Métis or who found such an identity unsatisfying. They appear to seek two things associated with Indians. One is to secure the special financial benefits which Indians derive from the treaties. The second is to be associated with the romance of being Indian. Often, they are those most desirous of dressing in buckskin and plumed head dress and dancing the newly manufactured "Indian" dances that are so popular with the public who flock to watch such productions. The spectators are pleased to see the "real" Indians. It is, one suspects, an escape from the disappointing reality of seeing on television the Indian leaders who act, dress and negotiate as do non-Indians. These leaders are shrewd, intelligent and forceful — anything but "quaint". As they do not fit the stereotype, the average citizen is often disconcerted by such modern Indians and turns with relief to the feathered and half-naked kind seen at dance exhibitions.

The manufactured "Indian-ness" of certain non-status young people perhaps helps them through a period of "identity crisis". Unfortunately, however, many of them appear to become anti-White, anti-Métis and anti-status Indian in an effort to convince themselves and others of their "true Indian-ness". To attract attention, they often degenerate into taking wildly extremist views based, not on logic, but emotion. As they are outspoken, the news media tend to devote an undue amount of space to their racist views. Such people embarrass both the Métis and the Indians and do a great deal of harm, for the public tends to believe that they are representative of all people of native ancestry.

The third category is composed of people who believe that unity of all persons of native ancestry is both desirable and necessary. The salvation of the people in an overwhelmingly White North America can be accomplished, they believe, only by building one strong organization. They not only see the need for unity in Canada, but also envision a pan-American union. In many ways, their views are idealistic and neglect the legal factors which are a basic cause of division. In another sense, the unionists are bluntly pragmatic. The myth of the "pure" Indian is challenged. It is maintained that the mixture of genes is so diverse that "Indian" should now be considered a cultural, rather than biological, group. The truth of this cannot be denied. It is on this important question that many Métis stand firm. The Métis are a mixture of race and culture, neither Indian nor White. They do not, as a group, wish to be either. They are what they are — Métis.

The Native Council of Canada tries to represent both the Métis and the non-status Indians. Whether the two groups can work together has yet to be proved. The non-status Indians wish to convert the Métis into Indians. The Métis aren't interested and resent the suggestion that they are Indian. Norval Desjarlais, a Métis who writes thought-provoking but humorous articles, has his newspaper character, Pierre Larocque, comment on the problem.

OBSERVER'S VIEWPOINT[8]

At Christmas time I visited my ole friend Pierre Larocque. Ole batchelor Pierre as you know lives way up north in his cabin. He gets kind o' lonesome especially around Christmas time and so I pack him a few pieces of Christmas turkey and the cheapest bottle of red wine and I visit him for a couple of days, if I'm lucky to stay that long.

It was a beautiful night and old Pierre and I stood outside for a few minutes and looked up at the beautiful starry sky. It was as still as only a cold cracklin' night in the North can be. A pack of wolves howled in the distance and ole Pierre howled right back. Way up in the sky we could see the red and green flashing lights of an airplane as it flew past.

"There goes Nellie again" ole Pierre snorted. He thought for a while and then he added "or it could be a community development worker — there's a lot of them around."

"Yah," I said, "if the Métis people had half the money them guys up there spend on community development — we'd all be rich. In fact, Pierre sometimes I think it would be kind of nice and cozy life if we could all join some Government Department like ah, — well say the Department of Indian Affairs — now that's something big and they've got lots of money."

Ole Pierre turned on me like a lion, steam belching out of his nostrils like an ole steamer — his eyes like fire.

"Wat you saying, Norval?" ole Pierre shouted at me.

He caught me by the shoulder and shoved me back into the shack.

"Who you think you are?" ole Pierre snarled at me — "you is ole Jean Baptiste's boy — dat's who."

Ole Pierre walked around the shack for awhile and took a couple swigs of wine. I could see he was mad. Finally, he took down his fiddle that was hanging on the wall and started to tune er up: zing, zing, zing, zum, zum, zum, zong, zong, zong, zong, zong. He played a few bars from his fiddlin' favorite "The old man and the old woman." "It's lucky chance for you, Norval, that your ole granfodder can't hear you now — you wanting to join the Department of Indian Affairs, get a number, and live on a reserve like Fisher River 1795."

"Ole Billy Fleury in Winnipeg he tell me now that George Munro, Archie Nabess, Joe Keeper and lots of udder good Métis guys now is saying "der is no such thing as a Métis — we is Indians.""

"Yah, but not me Pierre — not me!"

"The newspapers say that Mrs. Lavell from Ontario who married a white man is going to court and try to get her treaty number back again. Dat's ok with me, Norval, for she is an Indian. But what about her kids? I suppose the Department of Indian Affairs will give dem a number and that will make dem Indians. But what if dem kids should marry white people, eh?"

"By gosh Pierre, maybe we could set up an M.M.F.* office on the Reserves and they could join the Federation," I said.

"Norval, you crazy," said ole Pierre angrily. "When your granfodder saw the last buffalo being killed on the prairies he cried, yes sir, ole Jean Baptiste cried, — and now the Red man he's going too like the buffalo and you is laughing."

They should leave the poor Indians alone. Why in hell do George and them guys work in a place dey call the Indian and Métis Friendship Centre, if der is no Métis? Why do dey call their newapaper "The New Nation." It was the Métis who called demselves the "New Nation", not the Indians.

And look at Tony Belcourt, the President of the Native Council of Canada. He's wearing beads around hees neck and going around and maken' big speeches and calling all Native people Indians. Him and big Gene Rheaume of the Native Council of Canada, them guys write dat newspaper called "The Forgotten People" and its all about the Indians, nothing about the Métis, but its the Métis people who are forgotten, not the Indians. Its the Métis people who got nothing, no free education, no houses, no economic programs, no nothing except a kick in the ass and community development — dat wat the Métis get."

Ole Pierre was mad as hell now and his voice was so loud he wake up the cat who was sleeping near the stove and Pierre kicked him in the ass and sent it flying through the shack.

"Ole Jean Baptiste, you remember your ole granfodder, he use to say dat de Métis were the 'blue bloods of the prairies'. I tink dat ole' Baptiste was right. Our blood is not Red like the true Indians and not white like de whiteman's, but when mixed togedder de blood turn — blue. Now all the MIB** is got to do is to test the blood of everybody on the Reserves and when dey find somebody with blue blood — den out, out of the reserve — dat's wat ole Pierre say."

I bust out laughing — "blue Blood" ha, ha, ha.

Ole Pierre looked at me through squinty eyes and then stepped up and punched me right in the nose. I saw stars flying in all directions — white ones, red ones and blue ones. I picked myself off the floor and wiped my bloody nose. "By gosh Pierre," I said, "you're right, it is blue."

"Dat's wat I said," said Pierre as he took another swig of wine and finished off with a few bars from "The Maple Sugar Reel."

Pierre thought about this for a long time while he fiddled out a lively jig and kept beat with his feet.

Suddenly, he stopped and his eyes brightened up. "You know, Norval, your ole granfodder, ole Jean Baptiste used to tell me dat he could always tell de Indian from de Métis by de music. Sometimes at night, after a long days hunt, he would be walking across de prairies hungry and tired. He would see a campfire — 'ah mon dieu, at las' and den he would leesin, if he heard fiddle music he would go and he would be received with open arms and he would eat, and laugh, and dance and teekle dem beautiful Métis girls and den he would sleep 'appy, 'appy.

But if he heerd tom-toms, ole Jean Baptiste would keep right on walking.

So I say to you Norval, dat is how we should find de true Métis and de true Indian. Anybody who want to join the Indians den dey must first of all, do de war dance, snake dance, grass dance, and play de tom-toms."

"No Pierre, it won't work," I said quite firmly. "The Department of Indian Affairs said that blood testing was a very dangerous thing. It was contagious and could spread all over the country and then the next thing there would be more reserves left. No Pierre, that's definitely too dangerous."

"And all does guys who want to join the Métis Federation will have to do the jig and a square dance — dats the first thing before dey join — like dey have in dem secret outfits — you know what I mean . . .!"

"You mean initiation ceremony!" I said.

"Yah, Yah, dat's right," ole Pierre laughed as he fired up "Old John McNeil" on his fiddle and beating the floor so hard with his feet I could see the dust rising to the ceiling.

"C'mon you Métis guys" ole Pierre was shouting above the sounds of his fiddle. "Step right up and tamarack her down on the ol' pine floor."

*M.M.F. (Manitoba Métis Federation)
**M.I.B. (Manitoba Indian Brotherhood)

In an effort to unite the legal Indians, non-status Indians and the Métis who wished to become Indians, a new organization was formed in 1972, named the National Indian Movement of Canada. Based in Winnipeg, Manitoba, the organization stated:

"Speedy unification and nationalization of all native people is being pursued. We as Indian people are convinced that we have only one honorable course and that is speedy unification of all native people — that is registered or treaty Indians, enfranchised Indians, Inuit (Eskimo) and native people . . . Both governments and native organizations patterned by their tenents have a grandiose belief that they represent and lead the Indian people. The native organizations do not realize the dissension they are fomenting in the native community by their selfish intrigues . . . Racist practices are being "excused" by Manitoba and other provinces. The National Indian Movement intends to encourage united

173

confrontation and mass demonstrations to discourage the openly flagrant practice of discrimination ... The acquisition of education and monetary affluence is restricted to individuals and small elitist groups who monopolize positions in native organizations, Indian Affairs and provincial government pay-off positions, and on the reserve jobs and projects, which leave the majority of native populations on welfare . . ."[9]

Although the meaning is sometimes difficult to grasp, it would appear from the above quotation that the National Indian Movement will be concerned mainly with problems of natives in urban centres, since confrontations and mass demonstrations are hardly possible in isolated all-native communities. The established Indian and Métis organizations are based mainly upon the support of Indians and Métis in rural and isolated communities. Thus they tend to direct their efforts to problems encountered by people of native ancestry in such areas. Little time or effort is devoted to urban Indians and Métis. The National Movement may well orient itself towards people in urban centers. If it does, a vacuum left by the other organizations will be filled.

What appears to be developing is a new alignment of people of native ancestry in Canada. The Métis people have strong provincial organizations and will, in the near future, probably develop a national body composed of Métis people only. The National Indian Brotherhood already exists as a powerful organization. The National Indian Movement might develop as the spokesman of non-status Indians and those few Métis who wish to be known as Indians. Undoubtedly, the separation of the non-status Indians from the Métis organizations will be beneficial to both.

The following chart makes clear some of the differences in privileges and rights given Indians, Métis and non-status Indians.

ADVANTAGES

	Indians*	Métis and Non-Status Indians
Land	Tax free land reserved in perpetuity.	As for all Canadians.
Houses	For a minor investment of usually $25 he receives a free house to the value of $10,000.	As for all Canadians.
Hunting and Fishing Rights	With the exception of a limitation re migratory birds, hunting and fishing for food is allowed at all times.	Actively prosecuted by government even when hunting and fishing for food in isolated areas.

	Indians*	Métis and Non-Status Indians
Natural produce of the land	Vast wild rice areas on crown lands are reserved exclusively for them.	In competition with rich corporations for rice leases.
Education	Free education including fees and living allowances while attending university.	As for all Canadians.
Taxes	No federal taxes, including income tax, are collected on reserve property.	As for all Canadians.
Medical	Free medicine, drugs, hospitalization, dental and eye care.	As for all Canadians.
Employment	Discrimination in favor of Indians in certain Federal Departments such as the Department of Indian Affairs and Northern Development. Discrimination in other areas on the basis of color.	Discrimination in many areas depending upon color of their skin.
Economic Development	$25,000,000 revolving fund set up by the Federal Government.	None
Commercial Fishing	Some Crown owned lakes reserved especially for them.	In competition with rich commercial companies.
Law	Certain crimes are prosecuted under the Indian Act rather than ordinary civil and criminal law.	As for all Canadians.
Attitude of Public	Tends to romanticize them.	Wonders why they don't live on reserves.

*Not all the above rights and privileges accrue to Indians residing off the reserves.

DISADVANTAGES

	Indians	Métis and Non-Status Indians
Color	Visibly brown and often discriminated against.	Many are visibly brown and often discriminated against.
History	Negative image in history.	Negative image in history.

175

	Indians*	Métis and Non-Status Indians
Education	Curriculum oriented towards white society and often unsuitable for them.	Currciulum oriented towards white society and often unsuitable for them.
Language	95% have a mother language other than French or English*.	70% have a mother language other than English as a mother tongue.*
Household goods	Merchants reluctant to sell on credit because they can not repossess goods or garnishee wages if on reserve.	Class them as Indians and falsely believe that goods can't be repossessed so are reluctant to sell on credit.

*Estimate

Most Métis have no desire to acquire the special privileges that Indians derive from the treaties. But the examples used show why many non-status Indians are striving to become Indians in a legal sense. They also show why an organization comprised of both Métis and non-status Indians will almost inevitably be beset by conflict. The resolution of such conflict will require the most diplomatic leadership by present and future executives of the Native Council of Canada.

A major factor in the development of any organization is a stable source of funds. In this regard, the Métis and non-status Indians have been severely hampered. With a minimal amount of money derived from membership fees, the organizations have been at the mercy of governments that have not been excessively concerned with their problems. One year, a government will undertake to fund needed programs, but there is no assurance that money will be available to carry the program to completion in future years. Personnel are hired by the Métis to begin programs but must be discharged when funding is discontinued. In another year, funding may be re-established and new inexperienced personnel must be hired. Frequent staff changes hinder the development of men with leadership potential. Governments fund worthy organizations because they sense the vote-gathering power of such actions. Canadians generally are obsessed with the problems of Indians and indications that the latter are being helped is a certain vote collector. Most people know little about the Métis, so that governments find it relatively easy to grant minimal funds with full confidence that the action will cost them few votes. Indeed, the public will probably be unconcerned if funding is withdrawn entirely. A study of the following statistics tells the story and reveals the fundamental weakness of Métis and non-status Indian Associations.

FUNDING BY THE DEPARTMENT OF THE SECRETARY OF STATE TO SELECTED NATIVE ORGANIZATIONS.

Organization	Population*	Funds from Secretary of State		
		1969-70	1970-71	1971-72
Indian Association of Alberta	40,000	60,000	175,827	102,000
Métis Association of Alberta	80,000	nil	nil	141,000
Federation of Saskatchewan Indians	40,000	61,000	185,988	106,000
Métis Society of Saskatchewan	80,000	nil	nil	25,000
Manitoba Indian Brotherhood	37,000	60,680	178,437	106,000
Manitoba Métis Federation	80,000	nil	nil	26,000
National Indian Brotherhood	240,000	500	nil	80,000
Native Council of Canada	500,000	nil	nil	20,000

*Numbers of Métis in each province are those given by the Native Council of Canada. As there are no precise population data on the Métis in Canada these numbers can be assumed to represent an educated guess.

These figures relate only to the Secretary of State. They do not include ongoing grants to Indian organizations from the Department of Indian Affairs and Northern Development. These usually range from $75,000 to $300,000 per year. Métis Associations naturally do not have access to funds of the Department of Indian Affairs.

12

The Present Day
Métis

Most modern day Métis and non-status Indian people have little choice but to integrate as quickly as possible into White society. They lack the cohesive sense of identity that was developed amongst Indians by a tax-free reserve of land, a form of government and a set of laws imposed upon them by the Department of Indian Affairs. In addition, Indians tend to oppose integration and, in some cases seek to segregate themselves. Only rarely do the Métis Associations consider the possibilities of segregation. They are dedicated to helping their members enter fully into the mainstream of society. In the process of integrating, the Métis and non-status Indians are experiencing many problems which can be considered under four major categories: rural lands, isolated northern communities, migration to urban centres and housing. As an in-depth study of present day problems across Canada would require many volumes, this chapter examines only examples from various parts of the nation. In so doing, it relies heavily upon briefs submitted to governments by various Métis and non-status Indians Associations.

Rural Lands
To Métis people in rural areas, and particularly in the northern unorganized portions of the provinces, the question of land is a continuing problem. Squatting on or leasing provincial land offers little security since at any time other people or large corporations may enter into agreements with provincial governments for the use of the land, in

179

which case the Métis then find themselves dispossessed. In all fairness to governments, it must be noted that they often have no idea that people are squatting on the land and have been doing so for generations. If land is not officially leased, the distant bureaucrat assumes that it is unoccupied and feels free to negotiate with individuals and corporations for the utilization of it. The lack of a land base and the inability to gain one works great hardships upon the Métis. Not owning the land in legal terms (crown lands can be leased but not normally purchased), they are without assets and thus often fail to qualify for economic assistance under various Federal government programs such as ARDA and DREE. For the same reasons, they also fail to qualify for standard provincial and federal housing programs. The lack of opportunity to legally own land discourages the people from attempting to build better homes or to improve the land for more efficient use in agriculture and ranching. The uncertainty of a future is a major factor in the lack of effort to improve upon the present.

A brief presented to the Alberta Government by the Métis Association of Alberta exemplifies the concerns common to Métis and non-status Indians across Canada. Its sincere and simple eloquence testifies to the agony of a people kept landless in a country of which they were once lords and masters.

> This brief is being presented to the Government of Alberta by, and on behalf of, a group of citizens who came to feel that their backs are against the wall. These citizens have historically attempted to preserve a way of life socially, economically and politically distinct from the way of life adopted by the white majority in this society. Now they are faced with a vast range of pressures tending to strike away the bases of their specific ways. Not the least of these pressures is that on the land the Métis people have historically occupied.
>
> We as a people have retreated before the advance of white society for just over one hundred years in Western Canada. We now find ourselves with no further opportunities for retreat. We have accepted the necessity to adjust ourselves to the economic, social and facts of life in Alberta; to seek the training, skills and assistance that will allow us over time to move into the mainstream, maintaining at the same time as much as possible of our traditional ways and beliefs . . .
>
> Our history has been a long retreat before your advance. We have moved northward and westward since our attempt to establish ourselves as a legitimate political force in Canada when in 1870 we were defeated by the imperial army of your ancestors.
>
> The Treaty Indian peoples made their collective reckonings with your forebearers, and as part of their reckonings received land settlements. The white people who came to western Canada historically came for the land. Individually, many Métis over the years have made their reckonings with the dominant society and have thereby acquired stakes in the society

the same as those of most white people. Those of us represented here, however, are of the remaining representatives of a people who preferred an attempt to retreat and preserve their way of life to the acceptance of any terms of settlement. Historically, we have been formally landless, although we always considered that we had a moral claim.

On the record, our forebearers made a choice which, if not the best, was not necessarily the worst. The Treaty Indian peoples have reaped, on the whole, little but pain from their settlements with past governments. Moreover, and this is no small consideration, our retreat had its dignity as a fighting retreat. We have not forgotten Fort Garry and Batoche . . . the Métis people on the whole in Alberta have been a forgotten people. They have been, of all the racial and ethnic groups in Alberta, the people who have reaped the least of the benefits of social, economic and political advancement in the province, and who have suffered historically the most incredible levels of privation on all fronts . . . that privation has been closely linked at all times with the specific status of the Métis people with respect to the land question, and with the wishes of the Métis people to preserve a traditional way of life in face of the advance of white society into the northwest. Now that the game is up, now that there is no longer a possibility of retreat, now that we are accepting the need to come to terms with the predominance of white society and its norms and values in Alberta, our future is tied to the land question just as thoroughly as our past has been tied to the land question . . .[1]

There is nowhere for the Métis to retreat, for the dominant white society's economic, political and social ways are rapidly penetrating the hinterlands. Economic penetration through mines, pulp and paper mills, the tourist industry and the building of hydro electric dams is influencing almost all those areas of Canada that, a generation ago, would have been classified as unspoiled wilderness.

Letters received from community associations by the Alberta Métis Federation indicate the pressure felt by people in outlying settlements. In addition, the role of a government "Guy" can be seen as being a great mystery to people who have lived a simple and uncomplicated life up to this time.

. . . I hope it is never too late to ask for this big question. And I wish to get an answer soon. The problem is we Métis People of this little piece of land, in which we have lived for over 80 years. This land I am talking about is about 500 yards wide, where we live, and it is a narrow point they call it, and it is about ½ mile wide, maybe a little more. And we are 8 families living on it. And there is not one family in this piece of land that wishes to leave the Birth Place of all our kids. We have been paying our piece of land year after year, paying tax on it. Now there is a Guy coming once in a while. We would very much like to know what is going on our land. We only went to one man, but he did not really tell us what was going on. I think it would be right to let us know what he is going to do with our poor and very small land.[2]

The insecurity raised by the Government leasing policies greatly disturbs the Métis. They feel frustrated and helpless before the onslaught of rich and sophisticated white men.

> Why did the government give the authority to   Co. to lease land? The people living at   don't even know about the land that's being leased. Why didn't they give us first chance to buy the land. Now since we have no land we could be kicked out whenever they like.
> We hereby affix our names requesting an immediate investigation into the reason for displacing our people in favour of a man who does not live here and has not any interest other than pasturing his cattle on Government leased land. Thereby forcing us out of our settlement where we have lived all our lives.[3]

The feeling of a last stand can be sensed in the report of the Métis Local. Sadly, one can also sense that these Métis expect to lose. Because there is nowhere left to retreat, they have no choice but to remain even if the land is taken. The quality and degree of anxiety is conveyed by the following excerpt from the minute book of a Métis local:

> This meeting is about this land . . . We are trying to own our land. And if we can get this land we would be able to get better houses. We do not want to move away from here as we have stayed here for a long long time . . . There are enough people here to form a colony, so why would we have to move and look for another place to stay? We would be thankful if we could get this land for our own instead of whitemen who would only use it for pastures. We could use this land as much as the whitemen. Some whitemen are anxious to get this land for themselves . . . We are not animals. Cows are the only ones that are herded from place to place . . . We don't think we'll move even if we have to.[4]

Isolated Northern Communities

In the majority of semi-isolated areas of Canada the basic problem is an economic one. As long as the communities were few in population, widely scattered and composed of small independent business men (fishermen, trappers, etc.), a livelihood could be gained from the local area. As population increased, the pressure on resources became greater. Large sums of money had to be invested to harvest efficiently the declining resources and outside corporations began to move in. Because of large capital investments, such businesses were more efficient and governments tended to grant them leases and licenses in preference to the local people. An in-depth study was made of one such community in 1964. The following excerpts indicate the general pattern of deterioration in Métis settlements.

The people of Duck Bay are living "close to nature" and their income is in large part derived from exploitation of the natural resources. The biggest resource in Duck Bay is fish, followed by lumber. Others less prominent are fur, seneca root, berries, and game.

For fishing and pulpcutting, outfitting is largely provided by white entrepreneurs (mostly locally resident), and these men are also wholly responsible for the marketing of the produce. Hence, the local half-breed people are essentially collectors or gleaners of natural produce, and possessing insufficient equipment and no organization, rely heavily on others for taming the wilderness and converting local produce into cash incomes.

In spite of living "close to nature" there also exist some means of support apart from reliance on the natural environment, and these are now steadily gaining importance.[5]

Fishing gives employment to a number of Duck Bay men for six months of each year. Licenses are granted by the provincial government and are issued only to individuals, or to men sponsored by commercial companies, that can guarantee boats of a suitable number with a sufficient size of modern fishing gear. In certain years, one or both of the fishing seasons may be cancelled to allow the fish population to replenish itself. Fishermen from other areas compete with Duck Bay men for the crop while tourists take out an enormous number of fish each year. As the fish population is depleted, fewer commercial licenses are issued each year. Today, fishing no longer gives a year-round livelihood to any men at Duck Bay.

Some individuals and families migrate during the spring to lumber camps in the surrounding countryside. Pay is earned on the basis on a set sum per cord of wood cut. The lumber season lasts approximately one month.

Fur trapping was at one time a major source of income, but an increasing number of trappers together with the encroachment of agriculture have lessened the number of fur bearing animals. The decrease in the water level of the lakes and, subsequently, the surrounding countryside has caused the large marshes to dry up, so that the muskrat habitat has been ruined. A decrease in the price of furs has occurred since 1945 and few men now attempt to earn a living by trapping.

Seneca root is dug during the spring and summer. Entire families may "camp out" for several weeks at a time to collect seneca. Everyone digs the root — men, women and children. During a good season, a family may earn $300 in this way.

Raspberries and other small fruits are collected by women and older couples during July and August. A ready market is found with local merchants and nearby farmers. Often, the money earned is sufficient to buy children their school supplies and new clothing for the fall.

In 1964, Duck Bay had a population of 600 persons. In July, at the height of the employment season, 228 were receiving welfare payments. In 1970, the main source of income continued to be from welfare payments. Most residents had no opportunity to secure even part-time employment. Within one generation, the people have changed from being independent to becoming almost completely dependent upon welfare payments, because of the destruction of the economic base by over-population and over-utilization by people from outside the community. Inasmuch as welfare is a secure source of income, the attitudes of the Métis towards work have undergone a dramatic change. The Duck Bay study details some of the present attitudes.

> Some individuals have developed the habit of purposely seeking public assistance by pulling off stunts. Such "smart" manoeuvers are then made public, and never fail to bring amusement of a semi-envious "I'll be darned" variety from even those who disapprove. One man recently managed to craftily obtain a taxi fare to Ste. Rose, a hundred miles away, to see a doctor (he could not go by bus because his back hurt too bad), but instead of meeting the doctor, he visited many relatives, drank all night and came back with a trunkful of liquor which was later sold at bootleg prices.

> Welfare is an income that is sometimes preferred to other incomes because it is dependable and well paying.[6]

The researcher drew the following conclusions about the effect of welfare upon the people.

> As the recipients of aid are not aware of what the aims of this aid are, they feel no responsibility toward its use at all. According to a familiar principle, when an objective is presented to a group of people who possess no knowledge of its purpose and, further, feel no identification with the agency presenting it, they either do not accept that objective or use it resourcefully . . . In the "culture of poverty" where money does not happen to be viewed as an opportunity to be invested for an even better tomorrow, the finances are immediately squandered on the instant pleasures of drink and play.

184

Two comments may be made at this point:

> a) When money is not used in a rehabilitative manner (as it appears it is not in Duck Bay) it tends to produce a sense of security which is unreal in relation to the work-a-day world. In the present welfare programme there is nothing consciously rehabilitative at all. Vocational training in needed skills or an adult education programme may possibly be substituted in part or in whole for monetary relief.
>
> b) An attempt to help or "treat" the patient by advancing him money does not take adequate appreciation of the cultural effects of this act. Every individual is not merely affected by social conditions, but in turn affects social conditions too. Examples of non-work, and especially of dependancy in certain circumstances are emulated and become values which may rise in ascendancy within the value structure. When that occurs an enculturation process breeds a "welfare culture" highly resistant to attempts at change toward more productive livelihood.[7]

Six years after the study quoted, the only full-time employment for Métis in Duck Bay was represented by two school caretakers, one teacher aide, and a local welfare administrator. One man cut hair in his home, while several women did laundry and cleaning duties for the school teachers.

The researcher pointed out although many in the community seem content to be on welfare, a growing number are dissatisfied with this way of life. An increasing number of the Métis in Duck Bay are becoming aware that there is no hope in the welfare society the state has created for them. A realization has developed that the larger the cheque received from the government, the more they are enslaved, for the more they are given, the more fearful they become of doing things for themselves. As self-sufficiency disappears, so does the feeling of self respect. Many of the more aggressive persons leave the community and attempt to get jobs in northern mining camps or in the large urban cities in the south. A certain pattern of outside employment has developed in Duck Bay. Men or women leave to seek temporary employment but return home after a short period. Once they have been "out", they are rarely content to stay home. The attractions of the city exert a strong pull and migration occurs again. Often, however, the jobs secured are of a temporary nature and, upon being "laid off", a return to Duck Bay is made again. A desire soon develops to have permanent city employment, which is most likely to be secured if one learns a "trade". To achieve this, an effort may be made to upgrade academic knowledge or, if possible, a person enrolls directly in a community college in a large city. Without considerable assistance in learning how to work and live in an urban centre, the migrant often becomes discouraged and may fall into the welfare way of life in the city, or else return home, disheartened and dispirited.

Migration to Urban Centers

In the urban centers, the Métis seek good jobs, good homes and good education for their children. In short, a better life than is to be found in the rural and isolated communities from which they came. The definition of "good" differs with each individual. To some, a good home is one with running water. To others, a good home is a modern split level suburban house. Similarily, the concept of a good job may range from steady employment to a high-salaried position.

The economic reasons which push rural Métis to urban centers also dictate the areas in which they settle. Most can only afford to rent rooms in a slum environment. There, surrounded by other Métis, they readily find social acceptance. Acceptance of each other as individuals is extended and received. If one wears shabby clothes, the group understands. Unsophisticated English creates no embarrassment, as such language is the normal expression of the people. The lifestyle and culture will range from the traditional to modern Canadian. The latter is followed by many but, no matter what the lifestyle, a person will be readily accepted by all. Acceptance is the key word, for from this arises a feeling of "homeyness" which is comforting and familiar. Invariably, there are relatives already in the city and a loosely structured, extended family, composed of aunts, uncles and counsins, offers assistance to the immigrant. This family relationship, supplemented by friendships, often provides the migrant with his first room, board and money until a job is found. Naturally, such kindness is repaid when employment is secured and the sharing of responsibilities and duties of the rural Métis community is thus established in the city. Commendable though this may be, it creates difficulties for those who establish themselves in a well-paying job. Less fortunate family members or friends tend to live with and/or borrow from a prosperous Métis. Such demands often keep the man from improving his own housing, food and clothing. If he refuses, or is reluctant to share, he will be rejected by friends and relatives. The possible loneliness resulting from such ostracism causes most Métis to continue with rural sharing patterns. The sharing concept becomes a hindrance to the material advancement of many and often negates the dream of financial success that brought the man to the city in the first place. In addition, if a particular extended family group has not been successful in adapting to urban life it will be able to offer little assistance or worthwhile advice to the newly arrived Métis. Indeed any counsel offered may be more harmful than helpful. The tendency, however, is to migrate to an area of the city where the extended family has established itself as a rather loose social unit. The area does not necessarily have opportunities for employment, so the migrant may simply be moving from a depressed rural to an equally depressed urban center. Métis and Indian Associations across Canada have been concerned with the problems associated with migration. However, many of the provincial organizations are relatively new and still struggling with basic problems of organization and are unable to undertake studies or launch major programs to alleviate urban problems.

The most comprehensive study and proposal for action has been prepared by the Manitoba Métis Federation and endorsed by the Manitoba Indian Brotherhood. Entitled *In Search of a Future,*[8] the document is remarkable in its comprehensive proposals to modify the problem. It assumes that, since the problems of Native migrants originate in the rural areas and develop in urban centers, the only practical way to deal with the situation is by providing a continuum of services beginning in the rural and isolated communities and carrying through to the urban centres. It has four basic aims:

1. to assess and develop the economic potential of rural areas with a view to creating economically viable communities;

2. to identify urban growth areas to which migration by Natives might take place with a reasonable hope of success;

3. to establish a series of migration centers, provincial in scope, to assist migrant Natives in relocating to an area and job of their choosing;

4. to offer these services jointly through the Manitoba Métis Federation and the Manitoba Indian Brotherhood.

The study and proposal is a pragmatic and realistic approach to a pressing social problem. Its bluntness and honesty has created hostility amongst Native people, as well as White persons, presently well established in organizations offering services to Native people.

The desire to create economically viable communities and make the people self-supporting threatens the vast, complicated network of jobs created by the need to deliver government welfare and hand-outs to Indian and Métis communities. Self-sufficient communities would create unemployment for large numbers of professional and semiprofessional workers in the area of delivery of social services. It would be wrong to assume that only White persons feel threatened. Considerable numbers of workers of Native ancestry are secure in well paid government jobs and they, too, are equally hostile to changes which might disrupt their comfortable way of life.

The deliberate identification of economic growth areas and the movement of people to them is also a threat to the society presently established in such communities. White people generally do not wish large numbers of Native people in any one urban center because they fear that social problems will result. Mining town administrators say, in private, that no more than ten percent of a community's population should be comprised of Natives. Beyond that, they allege, again in private, serious problems result.

At present, the services offered to migrating Natives are characterized by a complete lack of co-ordination. No effort is made to provide a continuum of services. At best, the Friendship Centers and Church Reception Lodges, are referral agencies, while at worst, they are institutions that have become bureaucratized to such an extent that their unfortunate clients are secondary to the needs of the organization.

The migration centers suggested in the proposal of the Manitoba Métis Federation propose to provide a continuum of service which would attack the problems of the lack of adequate housing, finances, information, preparation for urban living, self concept and confidence, group identity, as well as the confusion resulting from fragmentation of social services. Cultural misunderstandings, inadequate education, low-level job skills and the ever present concern of discrimination would also be dealt with through migration centres.

Lack of faith in existing government programs is noted:

> In some cases, the only accessible program succeeds in polarizing the client's poverty situation. For example, the Remote Housing program provides for adequate housing, but no further provisions are made for the inadequately fed and unemployed client. No priority is established for those who seek to relocate to another area for productive employment. No criterion is established as to the economic viability of the communities.
>
> Other programs provide training only, with no provisions made to secure employment and relocate the family in a practical and systematic manner to ensure its successful adaptation to a new and possibly urban environment.
>
> As a result, training has become an end in itself — a job that leads nowhere. The increasing number of Native people caught in this "train-

ing syndrome" is a cause for real concern, not only because of considerable cost to the taxpayer, but also because of the cynicism and frustration that develops among the Native people as a result.

Too often, the Native person, in the absence of a co-ordinated program, will strike out unilaterally to urban areas in search of the benefits of his training, But too often, discrimination; lack of finances, housing and information; and the psychological and social pressures, prove to be insurmountable hurdles without co-ordinated outside assistance in all of these areas. Too many either return to their communities or end up on skid row.[9]

If such needs are to be met, the study suggests, the existing Native organizations are the most likely to do the best job.[10]

Heretical though the proposal has sounded to the various government departments, the greatest concern has come from the professions. The proposal, *In Search of a Future,* gives little credit to the vast number of professional workers presently serving the Natives. The proposal places emphasis on the ability of persons of Native ancestry, who have wide experience in lieu of academic and professional qualifications, to give information, guidance and counselling. It constitutes therefore, a direct threat to the job security of professionals presently working with Native persons. In addition, the implementation of the proposed centers would lessen the influence of the Friendship Centers and churches. These groups, quite naturally, have objected to the implementation of the proposals.

To date, because of the lack of financial support, the Manitoba Métis Federation has been able to establish only one Migration Center. Located in the Northern mining town of Thompson, the Center has been remarkably successful.

The Thompson Migration Center serves fourteen isolated native communities. All are characterized by a high rate of unemployment which in some villages approaches 90 percent. A worker from the Center visits each of the communities at least three times a year. Interested persons are given information concerning job opportunities at the mine, in service industries and on construction projects. Information about jobs and wage scales are given but, more importantly, questions of housing, furniture, schools, food and clothing costs, payroll deductions and a host of other details are dealt with. If a man is interested in seeking employment, Migration Center workers arrange for a job and boarding accommodations prior to his arrival. He is encouraged to leave his family at home while the new job is being tried out. Upon arrival he is "twinned" with a Native person who is successfully employed. The partner accepts the responsibility of making sure the new worker learns to use the transportation system, guides him to recreational and social opportunities and explains many important details — for example, the deductions from his first paycheck. If the worker does not react favorably to the job, the Migration Center will assist him in securing a different one. His wife and family are encouraged to visit Thompson frequently, in order to allow the family to develop a familiarity with the town. If, at the end of approximately two months, the man feels satisfied, encouragement and assistance are given in moving his family to Thompson. Help in buying or renting a house is given. Relocation grants are applied for to help buy furniture and the complexities of installment buying are explained to the worker.

Once the family has arrived, the Native ladies of the community move into action. Assistance is given in coping with and understanding the complexities of urban living. Budgeting, shopping, locating a family doctor, schooling, appropriate clothing, operating electric stoves, thermostats, automatic washers and dryers are some of the hundreds of tasks with which the migrating wife is helped. Children are enrolled in community clubs, hockey leagues, Boy Scouts, Girl Guides, etc. The adults are guided to an appropriate clergyman, invited to bingo games and generally introduced to a multitude of social activities. The purpose of all this is to make the migrant comfortable and at ease in the new environment. Care is taken by the Migration Center to foster independent action on the part of the worker and his family. The general pattern emerging seems to be that these services are no longer required after approximately three or four months.

The Migration Center building contains a kitchen, dining area, lounge, offices and a number of bedrooms. Transients who drift into Thompson are given food and a room until permanent quarters can be found. In offering assistance to persons of Native ancestry, the Manitoba Métis Federation's Migration Center makes no distinction between Métis, non-status Indians and Indians.

During the period of September 1971 to July 1972, 621 men were interviewed by the Migration Center staff. Of these, 463 were placed in jobs and 65 percent were still employed in Thompson six months later. The success rate is remarkable in itself, but even more so when it is remembered that no professionals were involved. People who had once been migrants themselves simply helped new migrants. None of the Migration Center workers have academic or professional degrees in psychology, social work or counselling. Despite the phenomenal success of the one existing Migration Center in Manitoba, there is every indication that provincial and federal governments will not support the proposal to set up similar centers throughout Manitoba and other provinces. Opposition from established groups that wish to extend their present system of fragmented services continues to be the significant factor. Such groups wish to help people of Native ancestry, but not to the extent that relevant and effective organizations be allowed to supplant antiquated institutions which are characterized by high budgets and low rates of success.

Housing

With the exception of one province, every Métis and non-status Indian Association places housing as its first priority for action. (Alberta gives priority to the land issue). Although Métis do not expect that adequate housing will solve immediate problems other than those of personal comfort, it is realized that the peripheral benefits are significant. It is one important element in the process of change.

> "Although an improvement in housing conditions does not necessarily imply an improvement, in the standard of living of the people concerned, a better living environment creates a favorable climate for the pursuit of further education which in turn leads to better employment and the desire for better living conditions."[11]

The process of change begins in the home and, to a limited extent, its spirit is generated by the physical house. The deplorable housing situation of Métis and non-status Indians has generated considerable interest amongst governments. Unfortunately, most governments have developed such unwieldy bureaucracies that they seem to be unable to react in an appropriate way to people whose needs deviate from the norm. With this in mind, the provincial Métis Associations have attempted to negotiate regional housing programs which will meet specific local needs. The land and building needs of a trapper will vary drastically from those of a fisherman or an urban dweller. So must the housing programs. Government programs are aimed at urban needs and, in addition, are dependent upon the client's possession of a considerable sum of money as a down payment.

The majority of Métis and non-status Indians are poor — desperately poor. In addition many, perhaps a majority, lack the educational background and personal confidence which allows them to deal with the paper- and detail-oriented government housing bureaucracies. The Native associations have attempted to overcome these problems by forming housing corporations staffed by persons who understand the practical needs of the people in various areas and who are able to simplify the legal procedures. The housing surveys of the Manitoba Métis Federation and the British Columbia Association of non-status Indians indicate the pressing need for better housing.

	Manitoba[12]	British Columbia[13]	National Average For all Canadians[13]
with electricity	75%	85.8%	98.6%
with telephone	52%	58.6%	95 %
with sewer and water	11%	69.2%	96 %

Overcrowding is a major problem for many Métis families. In British Columbia, 54% of the households contained five or more persons, while 55% of the houses had four rooms or less. In Manitoba 62% of the households contained five or more persons while 72% of the houses had four rooms or less.

ECONOMIC CONDITIONS

	Manitoba 1972	British Columbia 1972
Full time employment	36.9%	30.5%
Seasonally unemployed	15.5%	65.1%
On welfare	30.7%	not available*
Other (pension, partial welfare, etc.)	16.9%	4.5%

*It would appear that those on welfare in British Columbia were classified as seasonally unemployed.

Government funding of Métis and non-status Indian Associations for the creation of special housing corporations may prove too threatening for existing organizations with their well established corps of workers. Present programs have proved unsuccessful, but governments are often more willing to expend ever increasing amounts of money in an effort to expand existing programs than to spend lesser sums on innovative approaches.

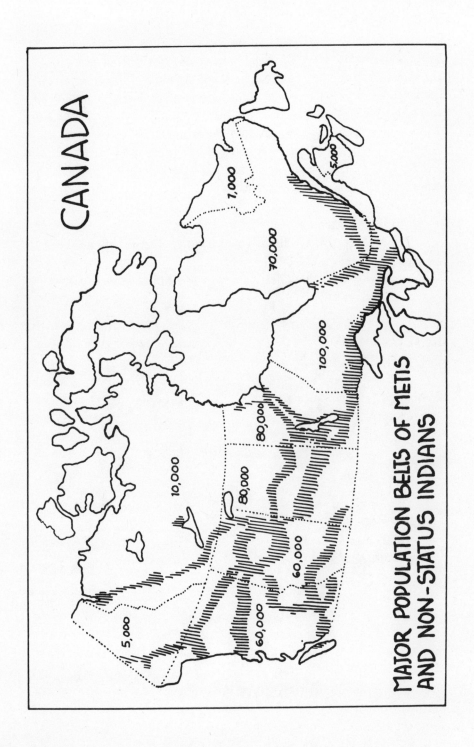

CANADA

MAJOR POPULATION BELTS OF METIS
AND NON-STATUS INDIANS

The Future

Governments must develop the ability to react quickly and effectively to the social and economic needs of the Métis. Failure to do so may cause a significant minority in Canada to turn from striving to improve their lot by positive action to more desperate measures. If the rural and isolated Métis Communities of Canada are not to sink into greater poverty, immediate action must be taken. Governments would be wise to work through existing Métis and non-status Indian Associations for most effective results. The vast numbers of Métis migrating to urban centers have found that life in the city is rarely better.

The deplorable social and economic conditions existing will, unless corrected, lead inevitably to racial violence in the many parts of Canada.

For there is no place left to which the Métis can retreat.

NOTES

CHAPTER 1:

[1]Geographical Board of Canada, *Handbook of Indians in Canada*, Printer of the King's Most Excellent Majesty, Ottawa, 1913. pp. 306-307.

[2]D. Wilson, *Prehistoric Man*, Third edition, Vol. 2, Macmillan and Co., London, 1876, pp. 252-253.

[3]Hudson's Bay Company, Standing Rules and Regulations, 1835. 42nd: That all Officers and servants of the company having women and children, and wishing to leave the same in the country on their retirement therefrom, be required to make provision for their future maintenance, more particularily for that of the children, as circumstances may reasonably warrant, and the means of the individual permit; that all those desirous of the same from the country not be allowed to take a woman without binding himself down to such reasonable provision and maintenance for her and her children, in the event of the issue, as on a fair and equitable principle may be considered necessary, not only during his residence in the country, but after his departure therefrom.

[4]D. B. Sealey, and V. J. Kirkness, *Indians Without Tipis*. Book Society of Canada, Box 200, Agincourt, Ontario, 1973, pp. 21, 22.

CHAPTER 2:

[1]G. Bryce, *Intrusive Ethnological Types in Rupert's Land,* Canadian Pamphlets, 1871-1913, Royal Society of Canada, 1903.

[2]*Ibid.*

[3]H. M. Robinson, *The Great Fur Trade,* G. P. Putnam's Sons, New York, 1879, pp. 231-32.

[4]*Ibid.*, p. 29.

[5]*Ibid.*, pp. 229-230.

[6]*Ibid.*, pp. 45-46.

[7]*Ibid.*, p. 47.

[8]D. Hill, *The Opening of the Canadian West*, Heinmann, London, 1967, p. 178.

[9]J. K. Howard, *The Strange Empire of Louis Riel*, William Morrow and Company, New York, 1959, p. 53.

[10]J. Franklin, *Narrative, 1819-22*. London, 1824, p. 73.

[11]F. H. Schofield, *The Story of Manitoba*, S. J. Clarke Co., Toronto, 1906, p. 145.

CHAPTER 3:

[1]Public Archives of Manitoba, *Fidler's Journal*. June 25, 1815, (Selkirk Papers).

[2]Public Archives of Manitoba, *James Sutherland Narrative,* (Selkirk Papers).

[3]*Ibid.*

[4]Public Archives of Manitoba, *Red River Papers*, J. B. Coltman to Governor Sherbrooke, p. 188.

[5]M. A. MacLeod, *Songs of Old Manitoba*. Ryerson Press Toronto, 1959, pp. 7-9.

[6]Archives of the Hudson's Bay Company, London, *Simpson Papers,* File 17, Copy in the Public Archives of Manitoba.

[7]A. Ross, *The Red River Settlement, Its Rise, Progress and Present State,* London, 1856, Smith Elder Co., p. 236.

[8]Archives de l'Archeveche de St. Boniface, *Correspondence de Divers officers,* No. 2, Macdonnell to Plessis, April 4, 1816 (translated).

CHAPTER 4:

[1]During this period the distinction between the French and English half-breeds began to blur as people from the two groups intermarried. Cuthbert Grant, a Scottish half-breed married a French-half-breed as did John Bruce, the first President of the Provisional Government. As the

language difference began to wane the intense missionary activity created a new division — Protestant and Roman Catholic.

²*Op. Cit., The Red River Settlement,* a remarkable in-depth account of the buffalo hunting expeditions is given in Chapter XVIII.

³*Op. Cit., The Red River Settlement,* p. 249.

⁴W. L. Morton, "The Battle of the Grand Coteau," *Historical and Scientific Society of Manitoba,* Series, 111, Number 16. A fully documented account appears in these transactions.

⁵Mgr. Taché, *Une Esquisse sur le Nord-Ouest,* Beauchemin et fils, Montreal, 1870, pp. 99-107, (translation).

⁶Interview, 1973, with N. Lussier of Winnipeg, Manitoba.

⁷Interview, 1973, with J. Lussier of St. Eustache, Manitoba.

⁸For a detailed examination of land grant problems see Martin, A., *Hudson's Bay Company's Land Tenures,* William Clowes and Sons Limited, London, England, 1898.

⁹*Ibid.*

CHAPTER 5:

¹"The General Report on the Progress of the Red River Expedition — 1859," *Smithsonian Institute Report,* p. 23.

²*Ibid.,* p. 24.

³*Ibid.,* p. 24.

CHAPTER 6:

¹Public Archives of Manitoba, *Riel Papers,* Riel to Taché, July 24, 1885.

²Charles Mair was one of the most intensely disliked Canadians in the Settlement. A poet and scholar from Ontario, he was appointed paymaster of a crew building a road connecting Canada with the Northwest. In addition to being a crony of Schultz, he angered the Settlement by writing a series of letters which were published in several Ontario Newspapers. The rude and distasteful remarks concerning the Métis enraged all members of the Settlement. Mrs. Bannatyne horsewhipped him on the main street of the Settlement for his remarks concerning the women. From the Mair incident onwards, the half-breeds were hostile to all Canadians.

³R. E. Sandborn, "The United States and the British North-West, 1865-1870", *North Dakota Historical Quarterly,* October, 1931, pp. 13-14.

Translation:
"Sir:
The National Métis Committee of Red River requests that the Mister W. McDougall not enter the North-West Territories without the special permission of the Committee.

By order of the President,
John Bruce
Louis Riel, Secretary

Dated at St. Norbert at Red River
This 21st day of October, 1869.

⁴E. E. Kreutzweizer, *The Red River Insurrection,* Gardenvale, Quebec, The Garden City Press, (1947), p. 20.

⁵G. Dugas, *Histoire veridique des faits qui ont prepare le mouvement des Métis a Rivière Rouge en 1869.* Montreal, Librairie Beauchemin, (1905), p. 192 (translation).

⁶*Op. Cit., The Strange Empire of Louis Riel.* Chapters VII-XI, gives a brief but interesting interpretation of events during the Red River Insurrection.

CHAPTER 7:

¹"Report of the Select Committee on the Causes of the Difficulties in the North West Territory in 1869-70, 1874," Archibald memorandum to Macdonald, October 9, 1871.

²D. B. Sealey, *Statutory Land Rights of the Manitoba Métis: A Documentary Study,* 1974, Manitoba Métis Federation Press, Winnipeg. A comprehensive account is detailed in the book.

³S. B. Steele, *Forty Years in Canada,* 1915, Herbert Jenkins Ltd., London, p. 76.

⁴*Ibid.,* pp. 276-277.

CHAPTER 8:

[1]C. K. Clarke, "A Critical Study of the Case of Louis Riel," (*Queen's Quarterly*, April, 1905), p. 384.

[2]Disputes sometimes occur over the use of the terms "Métis" and "Half-breed". Some contend that Métis means a descendant of a French-Indian mating while "half-breed" means a descendant of English-Indian. The record indicates that Riel considered the words synonymous. Examples may be found in the *Helena Weekly Herald* and the *Benton Record* of the period.

[3]*Canadian Sessional Papers*, 1886, XII, No. 43H.

[4]*Fort Benton Record*, May 7, 1880 (cited in G. F. G. Stanley's *Louis Riel*).

[5]*Ibid.*

[6]The Provisional Government of the New Nation was proclaimed on March 19 which was the feast of St. Joseph, the patron saint of the Métis.

[7]A gatling gun was the name given to a continuous firing gun now known as a machine gun.

[8]*Queen* vs. *Louis Riel*, Report of Trial at Regina, Queen's Printer, Ottawa, 1886, p. 134.

[9]*Ibid.*, p. 193.

[10]*Ibid.*, pp. 213, 214.

[11]*Ibid.*, p. 225.

[12]G. R. Parkin, *Sir John A. Macdonald*, (London, 1908), p. 244.

[13]*Op. Cit.*, *Strange Empire*, p. 468.

CHAPTER 9:

[1]R. Slobodian, *Metis of the MacKenzie District*, Canadian Research Centre for Anthropology, Saint Paul University, Ottawa, 1966, p. 12.

[2]*Codex Historicus of St. Albert*, January 29, 1879, A letter of Burgess to Honorable Clifford Sifton.

[3]*Chronical de St. Laurent de Grandin*, 1886, (n.p., n.d.).

[4]M. Giraud, *le metis canadian*, Institut d'Ethnologie, Paris, 1945, pp. 1023-25.

[5]Personal Communication from R. A. Logan, November 29, 1968, (excerpt from his unpublished genealogical study).

[6]J. H. Lagasse, *A Study of the Population of Indian Ancestry Living In Manitoba*, Department of Agriculture and Immigration, Winnipeg, 1959, Vol. 1, p. 54.

CHAPTER 10:

[1]*Op. Cit.*, *Queen* vs. *Louis Riel*, p. 47.

[2]*Ibid.*, p. 151.

[3]*Ibid.*, p. 153.

[4]The Indian Act defines an Indian as a person registered or entitled to be registered as an Indian. That means one who is descended patrilineally from a member of a band when the treaties were signed or the initial registration took place. This must be interpreted broadly as during the first generation following the treaties people moved in and out of bands rather freely. In addition many Indians sold their treaty rights or became "enfranchised".

[5]L. H. Lagasse, *A Study of the Population of Indian Ancestry Living in Manitoba*, Department of Agriculture and Immigration, Queen's Printer, Winnipeg, 1959, Vol. 1, p. 70.

[6]*Ibid.*, Vol. 1, p. 128.

[7]*Ibid.*, Vol. 1, p. 128.

[8]*Ibid.*, Vol. 111, p. 36.

[9]*Ibid.*, Vol. 1, p. 141.

[10]*Ibid.*, Vol. 1, p. 154.

[11]*Ibid.*, Vol. 1, p. 153.

[12]Public Archives of Manitoba, *The Emerson Journal*, Editorial, Friday, October 24, 1958.

[13]Public Archives of Manitoba, *Minutes of the meeting of the trustees of Neelin S.D., Sept. 14, 1953*.

[14]F. J. G. Dallyn, and F. G. Earle, "A Study of the Attitudes Towards Indians and People of Indian Descent", Canadian Council of Christians and Jews Inc., (mimeographed) Winnipeg,

1958.

[15]*Op. Cit., Indians Without Tipis*, pp. 129, 130.

CHAPTER 11:

[1]*Manitoba Métis Federation News*, January, 1973, Manitoba Métis Federation, Vol. 1, Issue 5, p. 4.

[2]Cardinal, H., *The Unjust Society*, M. G. Hurtig Ltd., Edmonton, 1969, p. 105.

[3]*Op. Cit., Manitoba Metis Federation News*, p. 4.

[4]Native Council of Canada, *The Forgotten People*, Ottawa, 1972, p. 7.

[5]*Ibid.*, p. 6.

[6]Human Rights Commission, "Report of the Total Commission", Winnipeg, 1972, p. 52.

[7]H. B. Hawthorn, (ed.) *A Survey of the Contemporary Indians of Canada*. 1966, Vol. 1, p. 266.

[8]*Op. Cit., Manitoba Metis Federation News*, p. 14.

[9]*The New Nation*, January, 1973, 590 Main Street, Winnipeg, Vol. 1, Number 2.

CHAPTER 12:

[1]Métis Association of Alberta, "The Métis People and the Land Question in Alberta", March 24, 1971, (mimeographed) pp. 3-7.

[2]*Ibid.*, pp. 8-9.

[3]*Ibid.*, p. 9.

[4]*Ibid.*, p. 9.

[5]Government of Manitoba, Community Development Branch, *Duck Bay*, 1964, (mimeographed) p. 9.

[6]*Ibid.*, p. 6.

[7]*Ibid.*, p. 7.

[8]S. Fulham, *In Search of a Future*, Manitoba Métis Federation, 1972, Winnipeg.

[9]*Ibid.*, pp. 2-3.

[10]*Ibid.*, p. 7.

[11]M. Lipman, *"Conseil des Oeuvres de Montreal, Operation: Renovation Sociale"*, Montrèal, 1967, p. 173.

[12]Manitoba Métis Federation, *"Proposed Housing Program for the Métis Population of Manitoba"*, Winnipeg.

[13]W. T. Stanbury, *Survey, Summer 1971*. B. C. Association of Non-Status Indians, 1972, (A sample survey of 2173 families).

INDEX

199